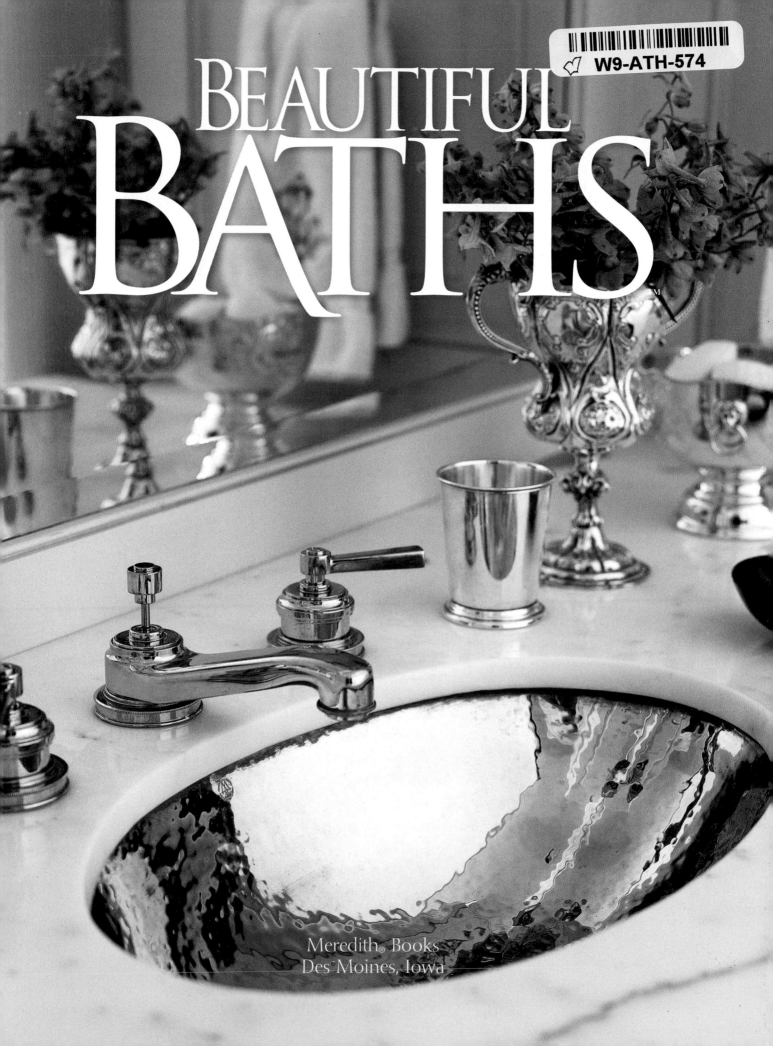

BEAUTIFUL BATHS

Meredith® Books
Des Moines, Iowa

Better Homes and Gardens® Beautiful Baths™
Contributing Project Manager: Jody Garlock
Senior Associate Design Director: Tom Wegner
Contributing Copy Editor: Rachel Lopez-Hohenshell
Contributing Graphic Designer: Mary Pat Crowley
Editorial Assistant: Melissa J. Caswell
Book Production Manager: Mark Weaver
Imaging Center Operator: Chris Sprague
Cover Photographer: Michael Partenio
Contributing Illustrator: Ann Weiss
Contributing Resources Editor: Marcia Teter

Meredith® Books
Editorial Director: Gregory H. Kayko
Executive Editor: Eliot Nusbaum
Art Director: Gene Rauch
Managing Editor: Kathleen Armentrout
Brand Manager: Mark Hetrick
Copy Chief: Doug Kouma
Senior Copy Editors: Kevin Cox, Jennifer Speer Ramundt,
   Elizabeth Keest Sedrel
Assistant Copy Editor: Metta Cederdahl

Executive Director, Sales: Ken Zagor
Director, Operations: George A. Susral
Director, Production: Douglas M. Johnston
Business Director: Janice Croat

Vice President and General Manager, SIP: Jeff Myers

Beautiful Baths™ **Magazine**
Editor: Karin H. Edwards
Senior Associate Art Director: Jack Murphy

Meredith Publishing Group
President: Jack Griffin
Executive Vice President: Doug Olson

Meredith Corporation
Chairman of the Board: William T. Kerr
President and Chief Executive Officer: Stephen M. Lacy

In Memoriam: E.T. Meredith III (1933–2003)

Compiled from *Beautiful Baths*™ magazine
Copyright © 2009 by Meredith Corporation, Des Moines, Iowa.
First Edition.
All rights reserved.
Printed in the United States of America
Library of Congress Control Number: 2008937791
ISBN: 978-0-696-24241-0

WELCOME

Bathrooms are more than just another room in the house. They're places to rejuvenate–escapes from today's hurry-up world. It's no wonder, then, that so many homeowners have put their baths at the top of their priority lists, creating special spaces to relax and unwind. The rooms featured in this book, a compilation of some of the spaces featured in *Better Homes and Gardens® Beautiful Baths*™ magazine, epitomize luxury. They all have the hardworking features required of a bath, but in these getaways tubs, sinks, and faucets are art forms; surfaces are superbly striking; and comfort rises to the top with chairs for lounging and soft rugs underfoot. Each of our featured rooms is filled with inspiration for bringing a similar aesthetic to your home. No matter the size of your space, you can create a bathroom that takes you away.

The Editors

Contents

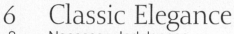

Classic

Elegance

*T*imeless, enduring, exuding tradition. There's a lot to be said for a bath that can stand the test of time. Whether you want to create an air of formality with marble and mahogany or cue a more relaxed vintage aesthetic with a claw-foot tub and beaded board, choosing time-honored materials and styles yields beauty for the ages.

Necessary

Style creates beautiful
function in this showroom
bath pairing durable
surfaces and intricate craft.

A bath is a marriage of contrasts, designer Brian Gluckstein
says. It requires clean, uncluttered spaces to function as a
calm oasis, yet it needs an ample dose of design polish to
appear more than utilitarian. "This is a retreat, not just a
bathing area," he says.

In this showhouse bath for the Kohler Ultimate Entertaining
Home, Gluckstein deftly played each element off another:
delicate, handblown Murano glass vanity lights and exposed
pipes; durable porcelain sinks and the gentle folds of fabric
shades; simple white tile and intricate marble mosaics.

The hand-cut mosaic follows a classic Roman composition of circles and squares in shades of soft jade green, blue,
and white. The design is set in a surround of white rectangular
marble pavers on the floor and repeats on the shower wall,
helping unite two zones into one dramatic focal point.

A freestanding tub with a deep ceramic base and gently
rolling rim overlaps the floor mosaic and establishes the
room's early 20th-century theme. Nostalgic fittings include a

Indulgence

This Photo: Mosaic marble in soft shades of green, blue, and white creates a "rug" on the floor and serves as wall decor in the shower.
Opposite: Tiny, hand-cut circles and inset squares repeated throughout the floor mosaic create an illusion of textural relief.

Right: Storage towers clad in marble subway tile and sited at opposite sides of the tub create a dramatic bathing alcove. Tile borders forming the cornice of each tower continue throughout the bath as a chair rail.

Right: Matching console sinks float against mirrored wall panels. The sconces are Murano glass.
Opposite: Mirrors and a floating glass counter transform a tiny alcove into a glamorous dressing area.

floor-mount faucet with a handheld shower and a pair of white porcelain console sinks. Eschewing contemporary frameless glass, Gluckstein chose a polished-metal-frame door for the shower, despite high-tech amenities including body sprays and steam.

As for storage, the designer makes a point of exposing things that add to the room's relaxing mood while hiding those that distract from it. Open built-in towers, wrapped inside and out with marble subway tiles, flank the window to provide space for spa gear and bathing accessories. Floor-to-ceiling closed storage, outfitted with drawers and doors, keeps paper products and toiletries at hand but out of sight. A mirrored niche interrupts these units to define a convenient dressing nook.

The design comes full circle with an adjacent morning bar, just steps from the bath. Complete with refrigerator drawers, a sink, and an espresso machine, it's the perfect place to start the day. "We planned the essentials," Gluckstein says. "Then we embellished the space with the ultimate luxuries."

MIRRORED SURFACES yield dramatic effects when sited with architecture in mind. Try mirrors inside an alcove or centered on a door or window—where reflections heighten the impact of symmetry and perspective.

Clearly Stated
Grace

A designer
envisions her
master bath
retreat as a sleek,
serene update of
Southern style.

Perfect symmetry and scale create drama
inside the understated bath. Vanity tops
and windowsill heights align as a horizontal
counterpoint to the tall bay window's
strong vertical impression.

Left: Dual vanities feature a shallow cubby at knee-height for comfort when standing at the sink. Sconces above are mounted directly on mirrors extending from counters to ceiling. **Below:** The shower occupies one of the six facets of the octagon-shape room. A glass shower door hides behind the paneled one. **Opposite:** Surrounded by carrara marble, the undermount hammered-nickel sink sparkles along with a few pieces of collected silver. All hardware—faucets, drawer pulls, towel bars, doorknobs—are also nickel.

Beauty, comfort, function. These are interior designer Jane Schwab's guiding principles. The relaxed elegance of the master bathroom she created in her 1923 Colonial home in Charlotte proves that she adheres to them.

Jane and her husband, Nelson, called on McAlpine Tankersley Architecture of Montgomery, Alabama, to design a master suite addition in keeping with the architectural integrity of the house—as well as its elegance. Jane also wanted a feeling of serenity in the bath, achieved with simple styling, including clean lines and smooth surfaces.

The bath is an elongated octagon, measuring roughly 13×15 feet. A bay of windows frames the stand-alone tub and creates three sides of the octagon. "The bathtub is treated as minimally as possible, as if it were simply a piece of furniture sitting in the deep bay window," says Scott Torode, the project architect.

Dual vanities line the two long sides of the room. The remaining three sides are the entry door and, flanking it, doors to the shower and water closet. These three doors and all walls are paneled and painted a creamy white eggshell.

The room's architectural strength cued its palette. "This bath is architecturally so pretty; there wasn't the need for a lot of color," Jane says. Nature also provides color through the views out the windows. Outside is a tumble of green most of the year, and at any moment something is in bloom, adding punctuations of color—sometimes soft, sometimes vibrant—against the lush green.

White surfaces make the most of natural light filtering through windows. Gleaming white carrara marble covers the vanity surfaces and the tub decking. More white joins the mix with classic subway tile in the shower.

Full-wall mirrors above each vanity also toss natural light back into the room, where it bounces off the white surfaces, creating subtle light variations depending on the hour and season. Above, a crystal chandelier sparkles.

The neoclassic-style bergère's creamy wash breaks ranks, ever so slightly, with the white motif. Handsome in raffia, it nevertheless sports a cozy, off-white cotton duck cushion. This is, after all, a room built on comfortable principles. ▣

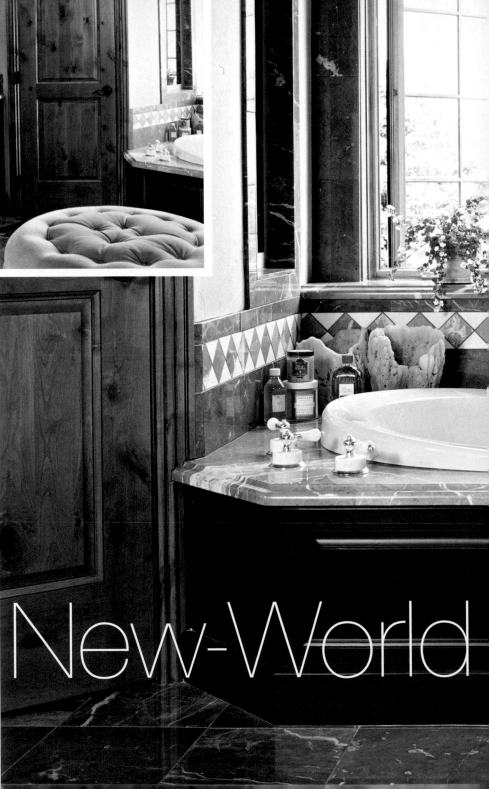

Red marble
inspires
old-world
elegance in
this rich
retreat.

New-World

Polish

Above: Tall cabinets divide a countertop to distinguish the sink from the dressing-area vanity, where a heart-back chair is covered in a fine quilted cotton terry cloth.
Right: Opulence reigns in the selection of antique-style, mirror-glass panels and elaborate silver hardware adorning cabinets.
Opposite: Stately cherrywood cabinets abut the fireplace wall, where the two-sided gas unit also heats the master bedroom.

Even before the new marble countertop was hoisted into place, the redesign of Nancy and Steve Markel's master bath was set in stone. At first glance of the earthy-hue marbles selected for counters and floors, the couple dreamed of creating an Italian-villa decor inside their Colorado bath.

Interior designers Judy Gubner and Colleen Johnson, working with architect Doug Walter, reimagined the space in handsome dark cherry cabinets, silver-finish hardware with the look of heavy sterling, and rough-textured amber-hue plaster walls enhanced by an umber glaze. "When Steve was offered options, he went for the more complex, more detailed choice every time," Gubner says. "Even for the plumbing fixtures, he wanted a silver finish—not chrome or nickel."

These elements joined a mix of marbles to bring an old-world aesthetic into fold with a modernized bath. The change began with significant demolition. Walter tore down walls to open the room into one luxurious space, with an oversize spa tub as its centerpiece. He reduced the number of enclosures by placing vanities at opposite ends of the room.

"I redesigned with balance and symmetry in mind," the architect says. He flanked the tub with a glass-encased steam shower and a private toilet compartment that can be closed off via a rustic wood door, which complements what is essentially a natural palette. "We ended up with a tonal scheme that includes light terra-cotta, taupe, gold, gray, and white," Johnson says.

Square footage gained in the remodel yielded one of Nancy's favorite features: a new, mood-enhancing double-sided fireplace. "It's particularly wonderful in the winter," she says. Embellished with a mantel and stepped hearth precast to resemble French limestone, it warms up both the bath and the master bedroom on the opposite side—a nice romantic nod to these soon-to-be empty nesters. "When you have five kids," Steve says, "you need a retreat."

The new bathroom gives the couple that and more. Cozy rustic touches aside, its look is as Gubner sums up: "Elegant, elegant, elegant." ⬣

Easy Meets
Elegant

An airy bath blends
cottage simplicity
with flashes of vintage
European glamour.

The faucet handles read "SHOWER" and "BATH" with arrows.

Above: Light bounces off high-polish fixtures, such as this floor-mounted tub faucet. The homeowner imported the faucet from Britain after falling for its vintage look and classic porcelain handles with antique lettering.

Michelle Hubbard expected the bath in her coastal California escape to be white, airy, and casual, but with a difference: She wanted to blend everyday comforts with her passion for off-the-shoulder elegance. Designer Lisa Butterbrodt achieved the mix, enlisting simple cottage-style architecture and classic touches of worldly refinement throughout: Venetian mirrors, carrara marble counters, crystal knobs, a French-style pedestal tub, and even a crystal chandelier. "It's a design oxymoron," Butterbrodt says of the combination of country and continental. "Matching elegance against such simplicity creates a yin and yang."

Having designed prior residences for Michelle, Butterbrodt knew her preference for vintage designs, clean lines, open space, and sunlight. In this new home, Michelle requested a country-cottage style, but Butterbrodt knew a plain clapboard look would not suffice, so she mixed simplicity with panache. The designer used furniture-style hutches and vanities that sit at varying heights for greater appeal and volume. Gleaming white carrara marble countertops unify the cabinetry and integrate well with the subway

Right: A minimally framed glass shower enclosure and white subway tiles add contemporary counterpoint to traditional, white-painted crown molding.
Opposite: Vanities on opposite sides of the bath feature Venetian mirrors aligned to create spatial illusions.
Below: A chandelier is placed under skylights for maximum shimmer.

shower tile and polished-nickel fixtures. "It's very luxurious," Butterbrodt says, "and doesn't quite feel like just a bathroom."

The room's synergy comes from details such as English-style exposed valves in the shower and vanities with soft, flowing draperies rather than doors. A white-on-white palette with touches of lavender on the walls ties the scheme together. "All the elements stand on their own and individually make a dramatic statement," Butterbrodt says.

The bath exudes a relaxed mood, in large part because of its airy aesthetic. To maximize the ocean light, architect Jim Gabriel combined vaulted ceilings, skylights, and wide-pane windows with painted millwork. Butterbrodt dressed the windows minimally and selected reflective surfaces–Venetian mirrors above both vanities, glass-front cabinets, and a collection of antique etched bottles from England–to bounce abundant sunlight throughout the space. Incandescent lights, including wall sconces used for task lighting, ensure that the room stays bright long after sunset. "The whiteness allows the outside to come in," Butterbrodt says. "It is very noncompetitive with the ocean landscape outside."

Other features enhance the room's restful ambience. The oval pedestal tub is deep enough for soaking, with floor-mounted faucets that evince vintage style while allowing Michelle to fill the tub to the brim with water. Thanks to a large westward-facing window framing the tub, a soak in its waters includes a spectacular view of the Pacific coastline. Curtains above are hung at Michelle's shoulder height, blocking out nearby houses but letting her see the ocean even when the panels are closed.

The oversize shower has an overhead rain spray to create a stay-awhile steam bath. Its sleek lines and clear-glass enclosure stand in contrast to the delicate vintage details elsewhere in the room. Soft crewel-on-crewel Roman shades on the adjoining paned window are just heavy enough to ensure both privacy and light. "We didn't want anything busy," Butterbrodt says. "It's all about simplicity."

Michelle's days are active, so she appreciates the tranquillity amid the glamour. "A bath should give you the chance to create yourself every morning," she says. "It should make you feel you are the most important thing in there." ⬥

Floor Show

Silvery blue softens a bath
where details take center stage.

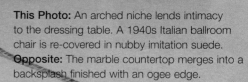

This Photo: An arched niche lends intimacy to the dressing table. A 1940s Italian ballroom chair is re-covered in nubby imitation suede.
Opposite: The marble countertop merges into a backsplash finished with an ogee edge.

This Photo: A marble tub backsplash is shaped for decorative effect. Fixtures add a gentle arc, echoed in the swag of the shades.
Opposite: Drapery panels soften the tall expanses of cabinetry flanking the sink vanity. Lines of silver-gray paint accent molding.

*T*heir story could be a Hollywood script. World travelers marry 19 years after they are introduced, then move to the groom's former fisherman's cottage by the sea. To ready the home, they add on, remodeling the master bath to fulfill the bride's passion for all things French.

The protagonists in this modern tale are Stacy Smith and Mark Gonsenhauser, who created Stacy's ideal bath at their Virginia home. Representing half of a his-and-hers bath suite, Stacy's space captures the elegance of old-world design. "I wanted a bath to remind me of the Ritz Hotel in Paris," she says.

The plans called for retaining the existing bath's footprint but improving the use of space. For assistance the couple turned to designer Irwin Weiner. Taking a cue from Mark's occupation as an importer of Oriental rugs, they started from the floor up. Stacy wanted mosaic flooring, but a search of various showrooms yielded little beyond small-repeat patterns and traditional border designs. Instead she desired a more free-flowing motif to introduce drama and a sense of play. Weiner ultimately designed the floor, drawing a leaf pattern based on a 1940s vase from Paris.

To fabricate the floor, Stacy and Weiner chose a pure white Thassos marble background and a blue-green cipollino marble for the design. Color striations in the cipollino were thoughtfully harvested to enhance the pattern, Weiner says. "We allocated the darker shade for shadow and the lighter shade for highlights."

The floor literally sets the stage for Parisian-style glamour, which Weiner finely balanced with soft touches. He eased the visual mass of floor-to-ceiling storage with the addition of seafoam-color curtains gathered behind glass-front doors, for example, and added a hint of silver to the cabinetry's white glaze

for a mellow, antiqued look. Then he enveloped the bath with the atmospheric effects of Venetian plaster walls for layers of subtle color, interest, and depth.

Other carefully selected details enhance the bath's goal of achieving the established, traditional look Stacy admired at the Ritz. These include the molding on cabinets, the carved backsplash of the tub and sink, the tub's casework surround, and the shapely feet of the cabinets and dressing table, intended to lend each piece its own identity.

"We didn't just buy one style of foot and apply it to everything," Weiner says. "On the one hand, pieces are stylistically coherent. On the other hand, they're slightly different." The same could be said for the two alabaster light fixtures, which Weiner discovered at a New York antiques shop. From the 1920s, they are similar, yet not a perfect match.

In the end, while the size of the original bath was retained, its architectural flow was greatly improved and its character enhanced to reflect Stacy's taste and personality. Calming colors and well-planned function provide a happy ending to the story, she says. "This is my little Ritz." ◙

Towering Beauty

An airy, classic master bath emerges from an underutilized attic space and now commands the best views in the house.

Opposite: This turret, original to the 19th-century shingle-style home, elevates the luxury of an oversize, jetted tub sited under its windows.
This Photo: Reflective surfaces such as the nickel faucet, antique Bakelite mirror, and silver-lidded glass jars emphasize shimmering light.

❝Materials are reflective, with a thoughtful **sense of history.**❞

DESIGNER STEVEN LONG

Builder John Lorang had a moment of design clarity while looking out through the windows of a gutted attic in this 1893 shingle-style Seattle home. As he stood imagining a master suite with refined lines and classic proportions, he recalled a quote from Michelangelo likening sculpture to an entity just waiting in the stone. In his mind's eye, he saw the deep, jetted bath destined for the room's window seat.

Siting the master bath to soak in better-than-180-degree vistas of Seattle's Space Needle, Puget Sound, and the looming peaks of Mount Rainier amounted to a total reversal of the homeowners' initial renovation plan, which called for a bedroom to occupy this space instead. But why sleep through such exhilarating views?

Designer Steven Long and owners Mike and Sumi Almquist soon came to the same conclusion, adding their own embellishments to what became a four-way design collaboration. The team arrived at a consensus on decisions so naturally that the renovation verged on alchemy. "Did we come up with this plan or did the house?" Lorang wonders.

Every element of the room is oriented toward the windows. Two custom vanity mirrors reflect Seattle's cityscape in oval frames while the roomy, glassed-in shower also offers unimpeded views from a more private vantage point at the back of the room.

But this is no sleek, cold penthouse bath. Empathy for the home's turn-of-the-20th-century architecture was critical to the room design. "I don't like renovations that deliberately try to look like historical reproductions," Sumi says. "But I also don't like renovations obviously out of sync with the historical nature of a house. This bath gracefully straddles both worlds."

Balance is achieved, in large part, due to the room's mix of contemporary detailing and period-appropriate forms and materials. For example, the wooden tub surround, with traditional inset panels, borrows its architecture from window seats found elsewhere in the home. The dark-wood vanities with classic marble counters are fitted with reeded-glass doors and curved legs more transitional in style.

"The bath has a fairly unpredictable mix of materials that contrasts aged surfaces and a polished, more modern feel," Long says, citing the shower's checkerboard panel of tiny travertine and iridescent glass tiles.

Long calculated the size of the shower stall in order to avoid cutting a single tile, thereby preserving the artistry of each tile's natural variations. "We were using quite exotic materials, so it was important to me that the master bath feel very well-crafted," he explains. Even painted walls aspire to this level of finish, combining traditional pigments with layers of metallic golds, pearlescent greens, peaches, and beiges. "When sun shines in, the whole room shimmers," Sumi says. "Then at night, when the city lights and fog roll in, it's simply amazing." ⬢

Opposite Left: Varying the counter heights and depths on custom vanities minimizes the cabinetry's visual weight.
Opposite Right: This mosaic detail mixes classic white travertine with modern, handmade iridescent blue and green glass tiles. The larger, caramel-green tiles surrounding them are also glass.
This Photo: Three checkerboard tile panels with ogee trim "hang" in the shower like framed artwork.

A sailboat's smooth curves and rich woods inspire the traditional style of a bath with ocean views.

Sea Worthy

Cabinets surrounding the Victorian-style soaking tub are framed in mahogany—a common sailboat wood—with mullions and panels of blonder bird's-eye maple.

Shingle-style Victorian cottages are no surprise along the shores of Long Island Sound. The style is an architectural staple that Jodie Bishop was determined to honor in her new home. "My husband and I are both enamored with shingled cottages in the area," Jodie says. "So we were very interested in keeping that same sensibility."

Architect Paul Harris, a longtime friend, eagerly accepted this charge to design a historically sensitive space—but with one caveat. The couple met in a sailing class and are avid weekend sailors. They wanted that passion reflected. Harris created a nostalgic design with materials and finely crafted details that resemble the interior of a yacht.

Custom cabinets feature rounded corners and an alluring inlay of mahogany and bird's-eye maple. The rich woods are paired with gleaming white marble countertops and a bank of glass-front doors draped with white sheers. "Sailboats often use a lot of teak and holly, playing dark versus light. That was the idea here," Harris says.

The sailing reference is subtle, while the design is overtly Victorian. The marble-top vanity features a wood backsplash with curved edges cut to resemble an 1800s washstand. Reproduction 19th-century damask-print wallpaper, hearty crown molding, and a porcelain slipper tub with shiny claw feet also create a nostalgic air tempered by white moldings and a contemporary feeling of light and space. "We wanted to re-create a house from a different era, taking certain liberties," Harris says. "The Bishops' master suite is larger than

Above: The soaking tub is centered on doors that open to reveal ocean views dotted with the sailboats that inspired the room's rich woods and custom millwork.
Opposite: A dressing table's lower counter and bracket feet break up the perimeter's expanse of cabinetry.

most baths from the Victorian period, but it aims for historical accuracy in other ways."

At the room's center, the soaking tub affords a direct line of sight down Long Island Sound. "We positioned the tub in the middle of the room for practical reasons, but as ideas evolved, its central location became almost symbolic," Harris explains. "It's more about recharging and recentering, which is something Jodie really values."

Jodie can soak in the tub, which floats on a sea of blue-veined marble, and look out to the triangular deck designed to resemble the bow of a ship and beyond to sailboats in the distance. Because of this beautiful view—or, rather, the radiant natural light it produces—Harris was keen to choose a neutral palette. Muted sea-glass shades of blue, white, and green offer a refreshing counterpoint to the dark woods associated with Victorian times.

"In rooms near the ocean, there's a completely different light," Harris says. "It's soft and filtered, even on a rainy day,

so we toned down the palette to exploit that misty quality." Delicate antique light fixtures dripping with crystals and glass cabinet doors lined with gathered fabric amplify such light effects with a mixture of restraint and grace.

"Many baths today have been dialed up, with enormous size and luxury materials as the focus," Harris says. "While this room is large, it reflects a simple aesthetic, which is a focus on the rituals of bathing and tending to oneself."

Maybe, as Jodie points out, there's ultimately very little difference between modern needs and an old-world point of view. "Bathing is a luxury," she says. ▣

Above Left: Silvery sconces include crystal drops for extra gleam.
Above: Bridge faucets featuring graceful curved spouts and cross-point handles with porcelain buttons provide period flourish.
Opposite: Sink vanities topped with marble blend into the cabinetry and are finished with low backsplashes in a style reminiscent of a Victorian washstand.

MIXING WOODS for contrast in hues and grains breaks up large expanses of cabinetry and accentuates details such as curves, panels, and molding.

Shedding Light on Tradition

Marble and mahogany make elegant partners, balancing cool whites and rich tones in a fresh but classic master bath.

This Photo: Traditional style meets the tropics in this renovated master bath, which uses rich woods alongside cool slabs of white marble, light-enhancing metals, mirrors, and half-height plantation shutters.

Opposite: The marble-lined shower is half-enclosed with frameless glass in keeping with the stately bath's open, light-filled look. Broad use of marble blends the shower's enclosure into the tub's backsplash and decking, as well as the countertop of a flanking vanity.

*S*unbelt climates almost beg for fresher, lighter-feeling interiors. Florida's love affair with whitewashed beaded board and wicker furniture, however, didn't pair well with the 1920s Federal-style brick home of Tampa residents Tara and Stephen Hood. Loyalty to interiors with vintage millwork—more traditional in Connecticut than the tropics—had the couple yearning for a substantial, sophisticated master bath. Yet Tampa's balmy days required that their bath also feel refreshing and cool.

Tara, a building contractor who specializes in luxury renovations, found the answer to her design problem in the classic marriage of mahogany and marble. Stained a dark chocolate brown, the bath's mahogany-paneled cabinetry radiates warmth against broad, flush surfaces of gleaming white stone. "I stayed in a Park Avenue apartment over 20 years ago that had a bath tiled in all-over white marble, and I've never forgotten it," Tara says. "I don't think there's any other material that has such a timeless, natural elegance."

With the materials chosen, Tara guided the transformation of the bathroom, once noticeably smaller than the adjacent walk-in closet it engulfed during the renovation. The new master bath brings a rich sense of tradition to the second story of a formerly nondescript 1960s addition. New amenities, such as a generous two-person shower, recessed tub, separate toilet area, linen closet, and individual vanities, assure that the vintage-inspired design stands up to contemporary needs.

The room's growth didn't stop with its expanded floor space. Pursuing a more upscale look, Tara had the bathroom ceilings raised from 8 to 10 feet. "We had to remove the roof and reframe," she says, "but without that extra volume, I couldn't have gone so dark on the wood or built those vanities. The result would have looked more like a den and felt like a much older, older bath."

In another move to lighten the bath's heavily furnished look, Tara designed the two vanities with features of an antique breakfront, including shallower cabinets on stepped-back sides. Above the vanity sink, triple mirrored panels reminiscent of a bay window bounce light and reflections. Inset glass shelves, recessed lights, and sparkling crystal and nickel accents further mitigate each unit's visual weight.

The brightest, most refreshing element in the bath's traditional scheme, however, is Tara's cherished white marble. Installed largely in slabs, the polished stone offers needed contrast in color, as well as texture and temperature. The sleek stone feels cool under bare feet and, seen against the silvery tones of polished-nickel fixtures, even its rich gray veining feels light—perfect for a classic, comfortable Florida bath. 🔳

Left: Mirrored backs behind glass shelves, recessed lights, and a triple vanity mirror work as space enhancers while fulfilling practical grooming needs. Crystal drawer pulls add the finishing touch, magnifying the light effects that minimize the weight of hefty crown moldings and recessed-panel cabinetry.

Natural

Inspiration

I Just look outdoors for inspiration to instill your bath with a sense of tranquillity. Vistas enthrall. Earthy and watery hues beckon. And natural materials, from rugged stone to warm woods, abound. The real beauty in letting nature be your decorating touchstone is the ease. Nature's colors and textures blend as harmoniously indoors as out.

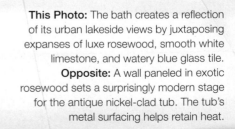

This Photo: The bath creates a reflection of its urban lakeside views by juxtaposing expanses of luxe rosewood, smooth white limestone, and watery blue glass tile.
Opposite: A wall paneled in exotic rosewood sets a surprisingly modern stage for the antique nickel-clad tub. The tub's metal surfacing helps retain heat.

Great Lake Modern

With luxe wood and watery blue tiles, this sleek space mirrors its lakeside setting.

MATCHING GRAINS from
one piece of wood to another unites
individual drawer and door fronts
into a strong graphic statement.

Right: The view from the tiled shower shows the bath's alternating use of rich wood, cool metals, and modern glass.
Opposite: A slightly curved front and marble top add elegance to each vanity. Architect Jennifer Knapp oriented the wood vertically, book-matching every piece to capitalize on a dramatically striped grain.

Light on the lake inspired Dorothy and Peter Marks to reimagine their bath in the 1920s home they've shared for nearly 20 years on Chicago's North Shore.

The setting is historical, but their bath is unabashedly contemporary. The marriage of styles works with a focus on vaulted ceilings, beautiful archways, and the overall drama of the home's architectural heritage. The "vocabulary of the house" and the lake itself, Dorothy says, dictated the design of the bath. Glass tiles in two watery hues (blue and blue-green) mirror magnificent views through French doors and windows. Expanses of richly stained rosewood are a natural complement to both architectural cues, complementing the home's tradition with the deep hue and adding a natural counterpoint to the waterside focus.

Architects Gary Beyerl and Jennifer Knapp planned a pair of curvaceous rosewood vanities, one on each side of the bath's French doors, and a floor-to-ceiling expanse of rosewood panels behind the freestanding tub. "We were going for the strong verticality in the grain," Knapp says.

The rosewood panels are flat and installed without trim to create a bold, modern backdrop for the lustrous nickel-clad tub. A freestanding European antique, it was refurbished and

Right: Glass tiles in three sizes and colors echo the reflective surfaces and varying blue-green hues of Lake Michigan.
Opposite: A shower bench contoured to fit a body's shape echoes the elegant curves of a sitting room chaise.

outfitted with a new Edwardian-style faucet set. "The tub holds you beautifully, the water is up to your chin, you gaze out at the lake," Dorothy says. "It's perfect." And the nickel sheeting retains heat. "You can fill the tub at eight in the morning, and it's still warm at night," Dorothy adds.

The tiled shower, a feature that graced elegant homes of the 1920s, takes a contemporary turn tiled in glass and has a modern bonus: It is a steam shower, complete with a chaise-like bench. The architects designed the bench with dips and hollows for maximum comfort when an occupant reclines

amid the steam, creating a contemporary ergonomic form. "We moved on to a modern look while staying in the right period of the house," Knapp says.

While the tub offers scenery, the glass-tiled shower promises seclusion. "That was the important goal," Dorothy says of the inventive floor plan. The design team provided for hidden yet convenient storage by way of two closets that hold towels and sundries just inside the entry. The paneled wall also serves as camouflage for two doorways—one leading to the toilet room, and the other to a home office. ◼

Set in Stone

A new bath invites its owners to meet in the middle with two equally earthy, modern spaces.

A glassed-in steam shower and tub become one seamless unit when joined by a marble tub surround that extends into the shower as bench seating. At either end of the communal bathing area are vanities, dressing areas, and doorways.

Funny how design changes by the decade, while some dicta never lose ground. Take the "form follows function" credo of modern design. In the remodel of this Encino, California, bath that was stuck in the 1980s—picture peach-sponged walls and mirrors everywhere—interior designer Nick Berman created an organic spa by flexing that most mature muscle of modernity. "Function becomes form," he says, "as the ledge of the bathtub runs clear through, from the tub to the glassed-in steam shower."

Indeed, the tub-shower ledge is the redesigned room's great divide. It stands as a sculptural feature in stunning Tasmanian gold marble, furniturelike, on four feet, and bisects the space into dual wings. The old bathroom had two sinks, but it didn't divide space the way the homeowners desired. For ultimate efficiency to accommodate their busy schedules, the couple wanted separate his-and-her entrances, separate toilets, and separate vanity and dressing areas, but contained within one room. Berman's behemoth of a tub/shower stall—one continuous element thanks to its ledge—was the start of the solution.

"The bathing area is the central spine," the designer says. "It separates the male and female sides, which are each customized for the homeowners' needs." The woman of the house has space for cosmetics, for example, while the man's area accommodates features like a television. A stereo system pipes in music for the enjoyment of both.

This Photo: With crisp geometry and organic opulence, a floating teak bench flanked by sugar pine sconces eliminates the need for more decorative features.

Left: The tub's gold marble surround extends uninterrupted for 12 feet, spilling into the shower as ledge seating. Tiny gold travertine tiles on the shower floor echo the hue and texture of the marble ledge. A handheld showerhead in an oil-rubbed bronze finish sustains the bath's Zen-like minimalism.
Below: Designer Nick Berman wanted the skylight beams to suggest ceiling joists, which would cast shadows on the stone walls and floor to increase visual interest.

Every inch of functionality is beautifully earthy. Flooring is teak, and several walls are clad in cashmere slate. "The slate transitions to the outdoor patio, for an indoor-outdoor feeling," Berman says. A skylight over the tub adds to that natural quality while illuminating the bath/shower space as the room's focal point.

For Berman, the skylight helps accomplish his dual-zone plan. "In addition to the change in textures that occurs here, there's a change in the quality of light," he says. "It helps the bathing area function as a demarcation element."

Materials are also key in marking transitions in the multi-functional room. Floors in the dressing and vanity area are swathed in ragged-cut slate in hues ranging from neutral gray-tan to rich ruby-plum, while the vanity countertops repeat the tub's monochromatic marble. One section of a 12-foot-long countertop is 6 inches lower to serve as a makeup table that never breaks stride from the free-flowing Tasmanian gold stone. Attention to detail and to comfort is constant. Slots between the teak floorboards permit drainage so there's never dampness underfoot. All of this translates as luxury, though not in an over-the-top kind of way.

"There's a certain opulence to this bath," Berman says. "Nothing decorative, but in the richness of the materials, which have such true warmth they create an almost sensual feeling. This, I believe, is how a bathroom should be: a naturally rejuvenating experience, where you create your perception for the rest of the day." ⊕

This Photo: "I wanted to create a neutral bathing area that would serve as an oasis for both homeowners," Berman says. "What's intriguing about the bath is that a couple can have their own spaces, then come together in this communal center."

Rustic Radiance

Invoking the charms of a French château is a matter of country architecture and formal flourishes.

Exquisite but unpretentious. That's how Lynette Pelligrini describes the allure of French country villas, the inspiration for her master bathroom. She and her husband admired how such villas layer elegance onto an essentially rustic construction, applying the raw materials of their countryside settings with uncommon flair. "It's that combination of comfort and elegance," Lynette says.

To achieve this balance in a bath remodel, the Pelligrinis enlisted builder Jan Kohl and designer Suzanne Hughes, urging the duo to remedy storage issues and improve overall flow in the existing master bath. Kohl and Hughes focused on creating distinct zones, resulting in a revamped layout,

VAULTED CEILINGS
add heightened perceptions of
space and a sense of grandeur to
modest-size bath corridors.

Above: Shower walls tiled in Jerusalem gold limestone add an earthy accent to the bath's soft, creamy yellow scheme.
Right: Wire door inserts and pretty drop pulls are among the furniture details that give the dressing table a French Provincial accent.
Opposite: Interior French doors mark passages within the château-inspired bath. This pair leads from the main bath area to a separate room for the shower and commode.

with the tub at one end, the shower and water closet at the other, and a vanity and dressing area in the middle.

Each zone is elegantly defined with architectural details. Vintage-style, arched double doors mark the transition from bedroom to bath. A matching set leads to the shower area, and a floating archway above the tub delineates this sun-washed corner as a separate niche.

Richly detailed cabinets line the long walls, creating a dramatic corridor with carefully planned vistas at either end. Lynette, once a draftsperson by occupation, was intimately involved in their design. She sketched the cabinets herself, eager to pay homage to the freestanding furniture of traditional French bathrooms but unwilling to sacrifice precious floor space. The shapely, antique-style built-ins that Lynette envisioned feature an abundance of storage, yet rival individual furniture pieces with varying depths and country French details. The dressing table, with an arched pediment and flanking cupboards, is especially dressy and versatile.

All cabinets are coated in a subtle caramel-tinted glaze, which Lynette developed with a local artist to create a feeling of age and authenticity. The special finish complements the general palette—whispering creams, whites, and buttery yellows. Cypress planks (on floor and ceiling) and nearly translucent honey onyx countertops offer a sense of cohesion and harmony. Genuine French antiques—such as the handsome over-sink mirrors and delicately scrolled light fixtures—round out the decor.

Graced with a lofty ceiling, abundant natural light, and personality to spare, the bath proves that old-world elegance can rendezvous with the conveniences of modern life. ◼

This Photo: A thick slab of travertine defines the double vanity. Walls and floors are tiled in the same stone for a serene effect.
Opposite: The bath leads to a deck, where an outdoor shower is screened on one side and left open to south-facing coastal views.

Second Nature

An indoor–outdoor spa bath is a serene extension of coastal hues and textures.

Left: Travertine tiles vary in shape and size within the shower. Long, thin rectangular cuts cleverly wrap curves.
Opposite: The tub is chiseled from solid granite—roughly finished on the exterior with a deftly smoothed lip and interior. Weighing 3,500 pounds, it required additional floor support and a crane to lift into place.

Picture a bathroom clad in floor-to-ceiling travertine, with vaulted ceilings and sleek, frameless glass. For most of us, visions of cool glamour rise to the fore. In this Kiawah Island, South Carolina master bath, such luxe touches render something very different: a serene, spacious suite where modernism's deft lines, pure geometry, and discernible lack of ornament are softened by the natural hues and textures of the marshy coast.

The bath leads to a deck with majestic views of its natural inspiration, which, architect Skip Wallace says, explain the spare styling. "We were asked to re-create the unforgettable spa feel of a Barbados hotel," he says. "I had a Zen space in mind—simple and uncluttered, where minds are free to wander without getting mired in unnecessary decoration."

Travertine-tiled walls and floors create the serene backdrop. Aged cypress beams form both portions of the ceiling, an 11-foot cathedral over the shower and vanity and a 9-foot flat covering for greater intimacy over the tub.

Features are minimal but bold, rewarding the eye with unfolding sophistication. An 11-foot wedge of travertine is masterfully cantilevered to form the sink vanity, for example, while the shower is plumbed into a 7-foot obelisk. The tub is a massive scoop of granite, set under a window lined with woven blinds recalling the coastline's marsh grasses.

Spa amenities spill out onto a deck furnished with lounge chairs for sunning and an outdoor shower screened from neighbors' views, but otherwise open to magnificent vistas. Indoors or out, in this bath nature prevails.

In Detail

Coastal hues and textures are thoughtfully echoed in this bath's use of natural materials. The palette is limited— beiges, grays, browns, and whites—so as not to distract from exquisitely rich and varied surfaces.

Clockwise from Opposite, Top Left: Designer Kristi Haygood had the ceiling's cypress beams left outside in the sun for several weeks before installation for a "weathered, silvery, more outdoor look." • White cotton towels rest on an antique Indonesian chest whose earthy, dark brown finish adds a dramatic lowlight to the bath's neutral scheme. • Expansive coastline views of sand, tall trees, and marsh reeds inspired the choice of mottled beige travertine, along with darker brown and leafy green accents. • Faucets are mounted on the backsplash so they don't interfere with the pure geometry of the stone slab vanity with integrated sinks. • The granite tub's roughly chiseled exterior plays against smooth, sandy-hue travertine floors. ●

The Rugged Side of Refined

A wilderness bath celebrates raw materials with discerning restraint.

Left: The sleek, sculptural tub in a Seattle woodlands bath is theatrically lit by flanking windows. Fixtures mounted directly on the slate wall emphasize the tub's proximity to nature.

This Photo: Custom vanities feature cabinets crafted from sandblasted and blackened steel and smooth, dark wenge-finish wood counters.
Opposite: Unrefined Indian-slate floor tiles shimmer in sunlight.

Seattle homeowners and active environmentalists Mark and Sharon Bloome wanted a master bath to evoke the feelings of serene detachment gained from a minimalist retreat, yet they also insisted on a design resolutely attached to its surroundings. Enveloped in craggy slabs of slate and blackened metals, the couple's new bath embraces the simplicity of pure architectural geometry, with echoes of the wilderness outside.

Pitched on a steep wooded hillside above Puget Sound, the Bloomes' home nestles into a landscape their architect, Colin Brandt, describes as vibrant and slightly out of control. "Our goal was to play up that juxtaposition," Brandt says. The solution? A design serenely contemporary but none too slick.

Materials are organic in substance as well as form. The slate used on floors and walls shows clefts, bumps, and rough edges where stones have naturally broken. "We wanted to leave all materials as close to their raw state as possible—finishing them just enough while also preserving the visceral connection between indoors and out," Brandt says.

Cabinets were crafted from blackened steel some of it from a foundry and other pieces salvaged from local scrap yards. Opting for a raw aesthetic, no metal was polished or buffed. "Some of it is even pitted," Brandt says. "Here the processes of making steel and its erosion are keenly felt."

As unrefined materials brought the outdoors in, a change in direction extended the indoors out. "One day we realized the bath, as it was proceeding, was just too small," Mark says, "so we decided to expand the room a few feet eastward so the bath hovers over the garden." The addition provided the freestanding tub, an intentional centerpiece of the room chosen for its combination of crisp lines and organic curves, its own alcove.

Floor-to-ceiling windows sharply illuminate the alcove, while beams from recessed ceiling fixtures rake its slate-tiled wall for dramatic backlight. The result creates a veritable stage for the tub, to build on the drama of a minimalist retreat amid the woods. "It's the ultimate achievement of merging the outdoors with something more elegant," Brandt says.

Other, more subtle choices intended to offset the bath's ruggedness include the warm accent of exotic wenge-finish wood countertops—oiled and reoiled for protection and sheen—as well as walls covered in handmade Chinese mulberry wallpaper containing particles of stalks, leaves, and fibers. "The rich wood and tactile paper add layers of softness that, combined with dappled light streaming in from the windows, really completes the room," Brandt says. "Beyond that, there's no ornamentation here, no jewelry. The materials are the elegance." ◗◗

Above Right: A spacious corner shower clad in muted green Brazilian slate doubles as a steam room, with a built-in teak bench.
Right: Towering Northwest pines outside the window are mirrored in the tub water's placid surface.
Opposite: Pits caused by rusting give the new metal cabinets "a touchability, a sense of the passing of time," architect Colin Brandt says.

Grand

Statements

Opulence may conjure palace decor, but why not lavish your bath with like-minded indulgences? Exquisite detailing, be it a dramatic bridge faucet that gives the impression of Georgian pedigree, an intricately carved door, or silvery pulls in a classic acanthus-leaf motif, lend an air of distinction. With a few well-placed touches, grandeur is yours.

Bold and Beautiful

A new showhouse bath inherits the grandeur of the good old days.

Pages 80–81: High ceilings play to the drama of this showhouse master bath, where draperies and two stacked mirror shapes accentuate the vertical space.
Opposite: Designer Shon Parker likes to mix textures and products, such as the limestone floor and porcelain crackle-glazed wall tile. The subtle contrast works in an understated classic space. Pillows and fabric seating areas serve as softening touches.
Below: The glass light fixture, *left*, was designed to fit the grand scale of the space. A tile "rug," *right*, frames each vanity, giving the floor visual intrigue.

The big and beautiful bathroom Shon Parker designed for a Decorators' Show House in Atlanta has the heart of an old-fashioned ballroom but the modern spirit of contemporary design. He first saw the space in the framing stage, when the bones of the room already indicated the look of a diva. Accordingly, he sketched out the high-impact statement of the tub centered on the bay window, flanked by twin vanities.

"I wanted a classic style, but calm and serene," he says. He chose an oversize soaking tub for his center-piece. The vanities won their spot in the room with striking, warm dark wood and graceful concave curves.

But the most important elements, Parker says, are custom-built mirrors installed behind the vanities, with holes cut for sconces. "This space demanded to use its height, to feel open and tall," the designer says of the 11-foot-high room.

Round mirrors above pay homage to the architecture of the 1800s, when doorways were often designed with a circle above. The shape directs the eye of the beholder upward, taking advantage of sweeping ceilings. The black frames on the round mirrors and the privacy screens on the windows balance the area.

The privacy screen, created for this room, is the haute couture of window treatments. Enhancing the linenlike draperies, custom-painted glass panels made in Italy darken the lower portion of the windows "I wanted to use black standard glass, but the color wasn't as intense as I wanted it to be," Parker says. "I wanted that privacy screen to be a dramatic backdrop."

IN BEAUTIFUL STYLE

- ADD FABRIC DETAILS—PILLOWS, OTTOMANS, A FABRIC-COVERED BENCH, OR EVEN A SIDE TABLE WITH A FABRIC COVER—TO SOFTEN A LARGE ROOM.
- USE MATERIALS IN UNEXPECTED WAYS FOR DRAMA. A CUSTOM-MADE GLASS PANEL STANDS IN FOR A MEDICINE CABINET IN HIGH STYLE. ASK YOUR CONTRACTOR TO CREATE OPENINGS FOR LIGHTING AND PLUMBING.
- HANDMADE PIECES, WITH THEIR IRREGULARITIES IN COLOR AND SHAPE, GENERALLY CONTRIBUTE DEPTH AND WARMTH TO A SPACE.

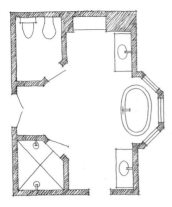

The limestone floor sports almost an Art Deco pattern, breaking up what could have been a cold, overly polished plane. Parker had the tile laid at a diagonal to draw the eye toward the center of the room. A tile border wraps around the room and bumps out to create the look of a rug under each vanity.

A seating area on one side of the space also plays to the room's height. Custom-made padded panels form the back to a bench nestled into a niche. The fabric panels soften a space crafted from so many hard materials. "I see this as a great place to sit and have coffee while performing your morning rituals," Parker says.

Artwork connects the classic design to the present. Paintings bring a bit of humanity to a room that, due to its sheer size, runs the risk of feeling overwhelming. Also, Parker says, "Sculptural art can really enhance the surface of a vanity."

It all plays off the diva charm that makes this new space one of the most impressive rooms of the house. ⬤

Right: While one side of the bathroom holds the toilet compartment and seating niche, this side houses a spacious corner shower and entry into a walk-in closet. The concave vanity fronts add grace.

The bath offers modern conveniences with a vintage twist, including a sleek shower stall trimmed in traditional molding, and a whirlpool tub cased in recessed paneling and fitted with a 1930s-style polished-nickel faucet.

Everyday Eden

A bath in a medley of classical materials interprets Georgian architecture in modern fashion.

THE MANY SHAPES a
ceiling can take—vaulted, arched,
or pitched—carve spaces more artful
than the usual rectangle.

This Photo: Requiring
incredible craftsmanship,
the unique shape of the
steam shower follows
an existing roofline.
Residential designer Kris
Boyaris elected to play
up its architectural drama
with traditional casing.
Sculpted edging on the
tub's marble deck echoes
such elegant trim.

Below: The exquisite detailing of a Georgian-inspired door pull with an acanthus leaf motif stands out against a sleek glass enclosure.
Right: Upper cabinets at the dressing vanity feature angled sides inset with mirrored doors. The wall-mount mirror is trimmed to match the molding in flanking cabinets, creating the look of a trifold mirror.

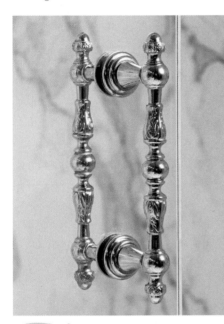

One might expect a pair of architects to make their own style statements when building new. But residential designer Kris Boyaris and her husband, architect John Krasnodebski, are very much "old house" people, even when it came to designing their new master bath. The couple drew inspiration from the crisp elegance of Georgian-style architecture, taking particular cues from historic homes in their Lake Forest, Illinois, neighborhood. "Traditional and classical—that's what we had in mind," Kris says. "And, of course, the bath had to complement the property's overall grandeur."

The bath is a spacious, handsome suite enveloped by woodland gardens. A wall of double-hung windows makes the most of such lush surroundings, converting the space for daily necessities into a sensuous retreat for lingering. Features including a stately encased soaking tub and glistening crystal lights add drama, but it was the windows, Kris explains, that guided the room's design and merged their historical inspiration with modern needs for space and light.

"In Georgian architecture, window expression is very important," she says. "These windows are positioned relative to the landscape and are really pretty organic." Set in a large bay, they surround the soaking tub on three sides, allowing for a unique, almost-in-the-garden bathing experience.

"Actually," Kris says, "you feel like you're in the garden from almost anywhere in the bathroom." This feeling is because of the couple's clever placement of multiple large mirrors and their decision to forgo blinds (which was possible because the site is so private). Lovely views are visible from the dressing table, double vanity, shower, and even the lavatory. The room's airy effect is amplified by light bouncing off high-polish surfaces, including nickel faucets, hardware, and a symphony of Calcutta marble slabs and tiles.

Below: Crystal sconces mounted directly on mirrors are reflected to create the illusion of a chandelier in the round.
Right: Polished-nickel bridge faucets add to the illusion of a bath with Georgian pedigree.
Opposite: Classical pilasters define zones at the double vanity—a division echoed above with three mirrors. Flanking upper cabinets are slightly shallower than the vanity, and conform to a pitched ceiling.

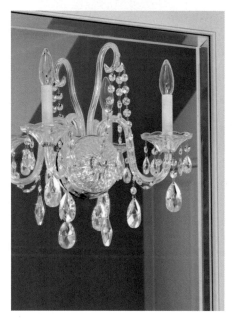

Kris chose a brilliant variety of white marble with pronounced veining, designating the most wildly grained pieces for the floor in 18×18-inch tiles. She used the same species of marble in slab form on the tub deck, vanities, and in the shower, designing a custom mosaic pattern just above the shower's marble chair rail. "Because of the bath's large size, we needed textures to be more bold and interesting, to fill up all of that white," she says.

Indeed, the suite is luminous in layered whites and taupe with extra glossy white paint on millwork to complement reflections off mirrors and nickel finishes. Kris designated wide lengths of custom-milled wood for all built-ins, not only to make a powerful statement with trimwork but also to better ground vignettes within the airy space. Individual stations, such as the dressing table with dual medicine cabinets, were designed to feel like stand-alone furniture, distinctly vintage in their styling.

The tub is included in her furniturelike designs. Kris had it encased in cabinetry to make it appear more weighted and substantial. "We didn't want it floating away," she says with a laugh. "And it was important to build some continuity and heft into that side of the room."

Ever conscious of balance and proportion, the couple chose delicate light fixtures to interject a counterpoint to weighty cabinetry. A finely detailed crystal chandelier crowns the space magnificently, while a trio of sparkly sconces mounted directly on mirrors creates a dazzling show of reflections. "The crystal, like the entire bath, is traditional but not too much so," Kris says. "They appear fresh and elegant, which is exactly the mood we were hoping to strike."

Vintage Deception

A remodeled bathroom gracefully hides behind a facade that looks centuries old.

Appearances can be deceiving. This bathroom looks like it might be found in an aging European manor. But it's actually the remodeled master bath in Barry Dixon and Michael Schmidt's Virginia home, where a few antique pieces impart elegance and surprise in the fresh space.

Barry, an interior designer, is a master at composing hardworking spaces. For his own home, he seamlessly integrated the functional details beneath a facade that looks at least a few hundred years old.

Reworking the previous owners' efforts to update the bath in the 1907 fieldstone country house included repurposing pieces, such as the garden urns Barry and Michael had plumbed into sinks, and setting the salvaged cast-iron tub on a concrete base to raise it to window height.

"We have the beautiful rolling hills of Virginia outside our windows," Michael says. "This base allows us to enjoy them from the tub."

Visitors would never guess the floor's tumbled Italian marble tile, used also as wainscoting, to be new. Nor would they think the old-world custom-made cabinetry had been pulled from anywhere other than a European manor.

The wall finish also joins in the art of deception. "I've been known to use things like cocoons as inspiration

Above: Latticework adds age and texture to the walls while allowing the mirrored surfaces to still serve their purpose.
Opposite: A balance of new and old fixtures and accessories helps pull off a comfortable bath with modern capabilities. The chair, kindling basket, and charcoal drawing around the hearth are vintage; the sconces, mantel, and floor tile are new.

Pages 94–95: Too high by most standards, the tub's extra height provided by the concrete base is no sweat for its tall owners. The bell-jar lantern is an antique picked up in London. Facing the closets and cabinets with mirrors adds depth to the floor plan's narrow dimensions and reflects natural light throughout the room.
Opposite and Below: A new garden urn that was repurposed as a sink blends seamlessly with an antique urn just a few feet away. A wall-mounted tap simplifies plumbing connections.

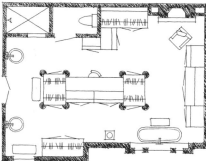

for wall finishes," Barry says. "In this case, it was the beautiful backdrops you'll see in fashion magazines that we brought to the faux finishers for inspiration. Old, decrepit European buildings—a patina that took centuries to achieve."

With his desired look firmly in mind, Barry started by dividing the oversize space into a bathroom and dressing room that would offer efficiency and modern amenities. He worked with bathroom designer Lois

Kennedy to pack function into the rooms without sacrificing beauty. "We started the process by analyzing our habits," Michael says.

Michael and Barry, both 6 feet 5 inches tall, ranked height-appropriate features high on the list of priorities for the renovated space. That's why the sinks stand a few inches higher than standard, and why the room's floor-to-ceiling closets are stocked with customized details. "We installed the closet rods high to accommodate

the length of our clothing, but that also makes them harder to reach," Michael says. "So Lois found a rod that lowers when you pull a lever. You pull it down to hang your stuff, and raise it back up when you're finished."

The beautiful final product belies the obstacles along the four-month journey. "Don't be dissuaded when something doesn't seem easy," Barry says. "You forget the pain, and you remember the above-average results." ◉

IN BEAUTIFUL STYLE

- SELECT FOOL-THE-ERA ELEMENTS TO GIVE A NEW BATHROOM VINTAGE STYLE.
- USE MIRRORS TO REFLECT THE VIEW AND THE LIGHT, A PERFECT WAY TO ENLARGE ANY BATHROOM.
- THINK CREATIVELY TO TURN GARDEN URNS INTO MEMORABLE BATHROOM BASINS.

Air of Antiquity

A bathroom situated in a high-rise disguises its contemporary bones in rich English style.

Left: Carved doors from a 19th-century French château inspired this bath's elegance.
Above: A pretty dressing area takes advantage of the light and views along one side of the L-shape bathroom suite.

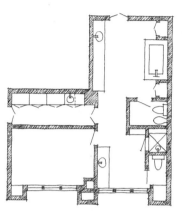

Marilyn and Lynn Elliott treasured the spectacular views of downtown Houston from the 27th floor of a contemporary building they called home, but a modern look just wasn't for them. Instead, they wanted their home to reflect the richness, warmth, and antiquity of English country manors, from the front entry to the luxurious master bathroom.

Marjorie Carter, longtime friend and interior designer, knew the Elliotts' style and was able to incorporate it into the bathroom with liberal use of exquisite vintage finds, specific spatial planning, and attention to detail. "The building had a definitive look," says Carter, who altered the initial layout to achieve just the look the couple desired.

Marilyn wanted spacious comfort, so the his-and-her floor plan includes a generous portion for Marilyn with a 13-foot-long vanity counter, thoughtfully divided between dressing table and sink. A pampering soaking tub, opposite the vanity counter, is framed by mirrored walls and billowing sheer curtains. Lynn's section of the bathroom is smaller and more utilitarian, but it enjoys perks including a deluxe, high-tech steam shower and extra towel warmers. Underneath, marble paves the way in luxury.

The visual highlight of the elegant bathroom is a pair of intricately carved doors. Once part of a 19th-century French château, the doors now lead to Marilyn's generously sized walk-in closet. "The doors were the main design inspiration for the bathroom," Carter says. "We took their beautifully carved details and used them to inspire, but not duplicate, the other elements we brought into the room."

Left: A relaxing soaking tub featuring English fixtures is a pampering treat interior designer Marjorie Carter repeated from a prior residence she designed for the Elliotts.

Left and Below: Accents, such as the painted dressing table mirror from the last privately owned estate on the Boston Common, add a personal touch to the wife's portion of the bathroom. The antique mirror was a gift from the designer.

Preserved in remarkable condition, the doors needed only a thorough cleaning to reveal a soft mustard/taupe body and deep-water blue highlights. A decorative painter replicated that original finish on all the room's new cabinetry, as well as on the warmly painted ceiling cove.

English antique or reproduction fixtures, artwork, and accessories match the style of the European doors. Crisp white fixtures, countertops of white marble with gray veining, and English-style hardware, such as the handheld showerhead and caddy on the tub, all enhance the English country look.

Carter is quick to note that any design inspired by the past requires planning and thought. "Things have to work well," she says. "It doesn't matter how true to the period [elements] are. They don't fit if they don't work in today's life."

That, she demonstrates, is the key to placing an English country manor in the Texas sky. ⬛

IN BEAUTIFUL STYLE

- INSTALL WALL-TO-FLOOR LUXURY WITH MARBLE.
- LOOK FOR REPRODUCTIONS OF EVERYTHING FROM PLASTER MEDALLIONS TO CABINET HARDWARE.
- ADD FURNITURE TO GIVE A LARGE ROOM A WELL-LIVED ATTITUDE.

Getting into Character

Classical balance brings order and elegance to a San Francisco bath.

Opposite: A 1920s vanity boasts a new reverse-painted glass top backed by a mirror.
This Photo: An old master portrait and large iron lantern hint at the surprising architectural grandeur of this small-scale bath.

Grand rooms can come in any size, as this snug San Francisco Bay Area master bath proves. Once a tiny, turquoise, and dated bath in an otherwise stately Georgian-style mansion, the room was revived by designer Martha Angus. "It's a classic English house, but the bath had an Art Deco style staggeringly out of sync with the rest of the home," says Angus, who suspects the last redo occurred in the 1970s. Her style-saving mission was to dig deep and repair at the roots, imbuing the room with character befitting the home's traditional circa-1930 architecture. "We took the bath down to the studs," she says. "Our goal was to rebuild with the symmetry, order, and integrity of the house."

First, her team eliminated a warren of small closets in the adjoining dressing room to gain extra feet for the bath. For a dramatic sense of approach, they built a barrel-vaulted ceiling at the bathroom's entrance. "The idea was to carry the English feel of the bedroom into the bath," Angus notes. The graceful arch creates a mini hallway ideal for a water closet and shower stall on either side.

"The barrel vault provides ceremony—a sense of unfolding," Angus says. "It takes you past the shower and water closet to lead up to the big soaking tub as a destination." It also makes the small room seem larger. But most important, the arch's stately paneling, which extends from ceiling to floor, disguises imbalances incongruent with classicism's insistence on symmetry.

"The shower stall actually occupies a much wider space than the water closet, but the paneling conceals this fact," Angus says. "It allows that portion of the room to appear symmetrical."

Symmetry, or at least a sense of it, continues at the tub, where paneled surrounds create a perfectly centered effect. (In fact, the tub is centered only between the surrounds.) At either end of the tub, Angus built storage cabinets for the homeowner's convenience. "She can reach in and get bath products without having to step out of the tub," the designer says.

Along one side of the built-in tub, a mirrored wall that doubles the perception of the room's size also provides a double dose of symmetry: Besides reflecting a pair of identical, symmetrically balanced vanities at the other end of the room, an antique portrait hung smack down its middle makes the mirror itself symmetrical.

"The homeowners wanted two vanities, but the room was quite small, so we angled the walls at the corners and custom-made vanities to fit," Angus explains. The result is a pair of rounded vanities with the grace and character of antique demilunes.

Below: Luxurious silver-plated faucets are sealed with clear lacquer to retard tarnish. "A little rub with a tissue" is all the maintenance they require, designer Martha Angus says.
Opposite: Faux-oak-finish paneling adds instant age to the dressing room. Two solid-hue carpets were cut into strips, sewn together, and trimmed with an acanthus leaf border to create a custom carpet.

"In classical architecture, everything has a central axis," Angus says. "It provides a cleanliness and order—a restraint—that is inherent in the central alignment of this bath's features."

In the adjoining dressing room, Angus changed the white-painted paneling to a warmer faux-bois (wood) finish. "We decided to have the whole thing painted to look like pale oak, in the style of Jean-Michel Frank," she says. Details such as this and reverse painting on the dressing table's glass top are finishing touches that make the space a timeless classic. 🛁

Sleek Sop

histication

Smooth surfaces, fluid curves, clean lines, quiet colors. These are the essentials of baths that embrace simplicity in design. Stripped of the fluff, every element, such as the arch of a faucet or curve on a tub, is sculptural. If you want your bath to be an oasis of calm, the uncluttered efficiency and understated elegance of these spaces will inspire.

The wall-mounted faucet on a shallow concrete ledge saves valuable inches of counter space while easing the transition from the smooth horizontal planes of the vanity to the vertical expanse of the tiled wall and mirrored niches.

Pacific Calm

Understated luxuries wait around every corner of this well-balanced, contemporary spa bath.

A mood of utter relaxation is what interior designer David Rivera had in mind when conceiving this luxury bath as a fusion of spare, planar architecture and earthy materials. While elements of its construction are high-tech and sometimes lavish, the design does without distracting extras.

"I wanted a room that is at once simple and refined so that when you come here to relax, there is not a lot of visual stimulation," Rivera says, "but where all the materials had a great tactile quality to them."

Built in a 1920s house as part of the San Francisco Decorator Showcase, Rivera's bath employs different surfaces, including limestone, teak, and mottled-glass tiles, to define three areas in a former laundry room. Plotted according to their functions are a mirrored vanity, sauna, and shower and dressing area.

Glass wall tiles run floor to ceiling, surrounding a concrete vanity centered on the room's longest wall. In defiance of concrete's visual heft, Rivera planned the vanity to float, unencumbered by cabinetry, in a niche created by the partition walls of a Japanese-inspired, two-person sauna on one side and a limestone-clad shower space on the other.

" Our intention was to create a calming environment from organic elements where **simplicity rules. "**

DESIGNER DAVID RIVERA

"I wanted tranquillity, so to that end, I made everything very orderly," Rivera says. "There's no chaos, no asymmetry."

That order comes through in the vanity's matching pairs of mirrored niches and sconces, as well as the floor and shower area's large limestone slabs—a necessary indulgence, according to Rivera—which, unlike tiles, require no busy-looking grout lines.

To deflect attention from such extravagance, Rivera relies on the soothing qualities of natural materials to ensure a sense of calm. Smooth, matte finishes whisper rather than shout; grays and grayish greens capture the colors of San Francisco Bay's waters. "It's not cold, but it's not warm either," Rivera says of the room's palette.

Artfully diffused lighting adds to the sense of moderation, while a few strategically focused rays build drama. For example, uplighting accentuates the room's 10-foot-high ceilings, and falling water from a niche fountain is illuminated to encourage contemplation.

Though contemporary in style, the bath's design did depend on one element common to older homes: extra-thick walls. That architectural asset allowed Rivera to carve niches, recess the towel holders, and build the water feature.

"It all makes the room look that much more custom," Rivera says, "which is eminently nicer."

Above: Up close, natural color variations in tiny, artisanal glass tiles appear as a rhythmic geometric composition. From a distance, the glossy tiles coalesce into one surface of subtle texture.
Right: The limestone shower is entirely open to the dressing area, where walls are troweled with a silky, green-tinted Venetian plaster, a compound made of limestone and marble.

This Photo: Water running over rough-cut, tinted concrete offers a soothing soundtrack to the nearby teak sauna. "It almost looks like an oil painting that has cracked over the years," interior designer David Rivera says of the recessed fountain.

Dramatically Inclined

Contemporary fittings and a classic masterpiece share the limelight in this intriguing space.

Left: A pair of French doors, original to the nearly 100-year-old house, never block the gaze of the Jan Vermeer-inspired canvas mural in this master bath. The doors formerly led from the master bedroom to a sitting room, now converted to the bath.

San Francisco jewelry designer Ellen Broadhurst's gutsy approach to life is reflected in her imaginative necklaces and the fearless way she decorates. The master bathroom in Ellen's 1908 Edwardian home pairs sleek contemporary fittings with a high-drama mural based on *Girl with a Pearl Earring*, a portrait by 17th-century Dutch painter Jan Vermeer.

This 15×15-foot bathroom had been the master bedroom sitting area. But nobody ever sat there, so Ellen decided to make the small bathroom a walk-in closet and convert this sunny space to a master bath. The mural wall had a pair of double-hung windows that Ellen removed, much to her husband's initial chagrin. The windows looked onto a neighbor's deck. "I knew a mural would be perfect there because the bathroom had another large window with a southern exposure," she says. "This was the perfect

Above: The quartersawn ash vanity features a marble top and undermount sink.
Right: Architect Steve Rankin designed the back-to-back tub and sinks to float elegantly in the room. A carrara marble-tiled partition between the two parts hides plumbing.

opportunity to block a bad view and create a gorgeous focal point."

Because the mural is so bold, everything else in the room is designed to fade away. "I knew that for the mural to be successful, the rest of the room needed to be quiet and couldn't compete," Ellen says.

Architect Steve Rankin agreed. The bathroom he designed is elegant and sophisticated, but in an understated way. Central to his floor plan and to the room's subtle beauty is an innovative back-to-back configuration of the whirlpool tub and a pair of sinks.

"I visualized it as a piece of furniture floating in the middle of the room," Rankin says. "It's designed so that the eye travels naturally across and beyond it to the mural."

Rankin proposed repeating quartersawn ash and carrara marble throughout the room. Ellen loved the simplicity and hushed opulence of the natural materials. "The light wood and white marble make the room airy and light," Ellen says. "It creates a real sense of calm."

The streamlined organization of necessities along the interior wall also lends to the sense of calm. Rankin tucked a built-in vanity between the shower and toilet enclosures. The entries to the spaces feature tall tempered-glass doors, and each area is illuminated by large skylights.

While the bathroom renovation was under way, decorative artist Lynne Rutter painted the larger-than-

Opposite: Marble tiles on the floor are used again in the shower and walls on the interior side of the room. The wall tiles are more heavily veined than those on the floor.
Above: The dressing table is quartersawn ash with a glass top. The area is framed by contemporary sconces and surrounded by marble.

Above: Large, new skylights bathe the toilet compartment and the shower stall in natural light.
Opposite: Homeowner Ellen Broadhurst chose to adapt a Vermeer masterpiece for this space because of the Dutch artist's use of light. Decorative artist Lynne Rutter also painted a true-size version of *Girl with a Pearl Earring* to hang in the bedroom. "I love the glow of his subjects and the drama and amazing detail that results from enlarging his portraits," Ellen says.

life mural in her San Francisco studio. "I kept the background dark to ground the airy room and make the figure striking," Rutter says. "And we located the figure on the wall so she appears to be gazing at you as you bathe, enter the room, or look down the hall toward the bathroom from the second-floor landing."

Once construction was complete, the large canvas (which can be re-moved if the family decides to move) was installed, filling the entire bathroom with richness, warmth, and originality. "Did I ever have a moment of concern that the mural would be too much?" Ellen asks, smiling broadly. "No way! I knew it would be wonderful. And it is. I never, ever get tired of looking at it." 🅑

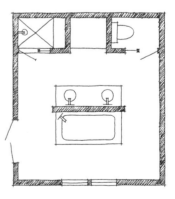

IN BEAUTIFUL STYLE

- PAIR A DRAMATIC FEATURE SUCH AS A MURAL WITH NEUTRAL BACKGROUNDS.
- VARY GRAIN PATTERNS OF STONE FOR ADDED INTEREST.
- "FLOAT" THE TUB AND VANITIES IN THE CENTER OF THE ROOM FOR AN UNEXPECTED TWIST.

This Photo: A restrained palette of warm mahogany and cool limestone enhances the serenity of this Asian-inspired bath.
Opposite: Smooth surfaces and clean lines define the two-sided vanity with sinks carved from limestone and chrome fixtures.

Turning East

Asian inspiration unites art and function in a renovated 1907 bath.

A thangka, a Tibetan painting on cloth, sparked Peter and Linda Krivkovich's passion for Asian art and culture more than 30 years ago. Since then, they've filled their 1907 home on Chicago's North Shore with furniture, bowls, and vases gathered on sojourns through India, China, Japan, and Southeast Asia. "These pieces fit well with our more contemporary lifestyle," says Linda, who had a similar aesthetic in mind for the couple's new master bath suite. "We didn't want to impose a style on the house," she says, "yet we wanted it to reflect our collections with something calm, Zen-like."

This Photo: The Japanese-style limestone soaking tub was built to provide extra-deep seating for two. Plumbing beneath the tub heats the stone steps while bath water is drawn.
Opposite: The shower and bathing area align with the room's central pagoda-shape double vanity.

IN BEAUTIFUL STYLE
THE ZEN APPROACH

- SIMPLICITY RULES. FOR A QUIET LOOK, LIMIT THE BATH'S NUMBER OF MATERIALS AND HUES.
- MAXIMIZE SPACE FOR EFFICIENCY AND FLOW.
- SET OFF COOL SURFACES WITH ORGANIC TEXTURES, OFTEN WITHIN THE SAME HUE, SUCH AS THIS BATH'S LIMESTONE AND FAUX-LINEN WALL TILES.

The Krivkoviches enlisted architect Ralph Hoffman, who found their Asian leanings to be a natural complement to the bath's traditional roots. "The nice thing about Japanese design and, in some ways, Chinese, is that it transcends many styles," Hoffman says. "It's conducive for very traditional settings, which this house is, and yet its simplicity creates a more modern, clean-lined look."

Because the bath is at the front of the house, Hoffman wanted the renovations to honor the home's century-old architecture. "We didn't want to touch the exterior or move windows," he says. Instead, he and interior designer Chris Garrett worked with the character of the space, accommodating old windows, chimney flues, and plumbing that couldn't be relocated. They removed interior walls to combine the old bath, linen closet, and sleeping porch into one larger, U-shape space, which they enhanced with shoji screen storage, a pagoda-style vanity, and rice paper accents.

Their goal in the bath's longer corridors was to maximize function without interrupting flow. In particular, they wanted to avoid having too many doors open onto the same space. "Every square inch counted," says Hoffman, who came up with several practical and elegant solutions. Extending the length of the glass shower to more than 8 feet eliminated the need for a shower enclosure; a sloping limestone floor contains water flow. Shoji partitions on a wall of Japanese-style mahogany cabinets slide, hiding daily essentials on shelves, in drawers, and in four tip-out hampers.

The most stunning confluence of art and function, however, is in the two-sided vanity island. Built of limestone and mahogany, it presents a pretty face from all angles of the bath. A recessed area at the side of each limestone sink keeps electrical outlets handy but hidden from view; thin vertical lighting strips eliminate the need for bulky sconces. "I like the way the lighting washes the mirror but isn't a feature," Garrett says. "We didn't want to do anything that would take up much room." As a finishing touch, a panel of burled ash tops the warm mahogany mirror. "You see that often in Chinese cabinets and Japanese furniture, which use natural woods in a decorative and expressive way," Hoffman says.

Ultimately, the bath's luxuries are both seen and felt. Limestone floors with radiant heat, for example, are one of Linda's favorite features. They make the room not only lovely, she says, but livable. ◉

Right: A corridor adjoining the bath was converted to a dressing room with stylish, space-saving sliding shoji screen panels on a wall-to-wall closet.
Opposite: The closet doors were made by gluing laminated rice paper to custom wood panels.

This Photo: A custom vanity in this master bath was needed in order to mount the wall faucets and hide plumbing. Rather than a backsplash, a horizontal crossbeam has its own through-view access to hazy light from a frosted-glass window behind.
Opposite: The vanity is topped with solid-surfacing and fitted with a round basin of the same material, providing a continuous and easily washable surface.

Spare
Essentials

A crisp, cool, and all-white bath is simply sensational.

With retirement on the horizon, Candace and Howard Broecker decided to simplify their lives—as well as the roof over their heads. At a moment when many simply downsize, they chose to build anew, opting for space but eliminating extraneous details from their home's design along the way.

The couple traveled to Japan, gaining an appreciation for the sense of tranquillity achieved through pure architectonic forms and spare detailing. Lessons learned translated to the modern glass-and-steel home they built on a bluff overlooking Lake Michigan, where their master bath stands as a dreamy white oasis against a backdrop of dense woods.

With the exception of bamboo flooring, Asian design influence is just a trace of an idea amidst architecture more reminiscent of 20th-century modernism and its celebration of geometrical forms. White was a traditional choice for such a minimally defined interior and provides the perfect counterpoint for the thick Michigan woods outside.

"I didn't want what's inside to distract from the views outdoors," Candace says. The sylvan landscape is visible from both ends of the symmetrically designed bath. Frameless glass doors enclose a roomy, porcelain-tile shower occupying the length of one wall, where a combination of frosted and clear windows plays with the seemingly contradictory notions of privacy and openness. On the wall opposite, a vanity is topped by a picture window in place of the usual mirror. Shallow medicine cabinets hang on side walls instead, and are fitted with mirror-back doors to ensure unobstructed landscape views.

Low-voltage track lighting, a feature borrowed from art galleries, sets a focused mood. The mesh-covered lamps can turn in any direction from a bar mounted on the wall above the vanity window.

Inspiration for the vanity's sturdy furniture shape came from a potting bench, while the steel towel bar mounted on the vanity's front is actually a pot rack. Open shelving below minimizes the structure's bulk, preserving the bath's light and airy intentions.

The only nonessential that Candace and Howard opted to preserve is the luxury of space, which amplifies the clarity of their bath's design.

"Someone once told me that as you age, you naturally gravitate to more contemporary," Candace explains. And now Candace and Howard's bath, with its breezy white design, fits right into their new, unencumbered lifestyle. ⬤

Opposite: Water-impervious bamboo flooring, with its natural tones, adds a warm counterpoint to cool white tiles in the shower. The transparent glass shower door and floor-to-ceiling exterior windows were planned to line up precisely, framing views of a wooded ravine.

Sheer Strength

Industrial materials and warm woods define a bath that is designed to last.

Left: The homeowners' daughter-in-law, a ceramics artist, made the tiles on the shower walls, and interior designer Jodi Gillespie found complementary recycled-glass tiles for the floor. Wood panels opposite the vanity hide storage compartments for medicines and toiletries. Frosted glass fitted into a metal framework gives the bath privacy while allowing as much light as possible to flow between spaces.

Long before this downtown Minneapolis building became home to lofts, it served as part of a General Mills flour-milling complex. The 1920s building no longer holds machinery and the pulleys and shafts that once defined the mill's inner workings, but architect Tom Meyer used its industrial heritage as the foundation for the design of this riverfront unit.

Meyer retained the loft's open floor plan in most of the main living areas, but he needed to define a more private bath area without losing the industrial feel that first attracted the homeowners to the condo. He started by building a structure from mill-finish steel to enclose the bath and adjoining closet.

"The metal framework was inspired by the history of the building," Meyer says. "It was a material way to give it that character." Leaving the pipes and ceiling beams exposed to retain urban grittiness and character, he installed frosted glass in the metal structure to provide privacy, without blocking much-needed daylight. "The idea is to let light flow through the space and give a sense of continuous space," Meyer says.

Within the bathroom, wood partitions lend privacy where desired, but most of the space retains an open feeling suited to the loft setting. The vanity sits in front of a glass wall that overlooks a small terrace. A short hall opposite the vanity leads to the shower and toilet compartments, as well as the master closet.

Concerned that the exterior glass wall in front of the double-sink vanity could easily become too chilly on cold winter nights, Meyer installed a large radiator system with pipes that circulate hot water in front of the window. "That grillwork keeps the bathroom nice and warm and toasty," Meyer says. "It mitigates the cold that would come off the glass."

To add visual warmth to the bathroom, Meyer and interior designer Jodi Gillespie included wood accents, choosing Douglas fir for its coloring. "Douglas fir has a golden quality to it," Meyer says. It was used as flooring

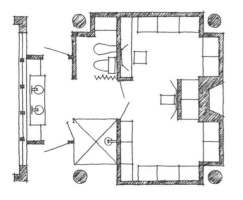

Right: Radiator pipes installed in front of the bath's large window and behind the vanity keep the room toasty even on cold nights. A mirror hung on metal framework was deliberately positioned a few inches above the sinks to allow natural light to reach the vanity area.

Opposite: The hues of the Kasota stone countertop and Douglas fir drawers on the vanity warm the industrial space. Chrome faucets complement the simplicity of white vessel sinks.
Above: Douglas fir slats top the closet and lend a sense of coziness. Track lights can provide extra task lighting or be reflected off the mirror for a more muted effect.

throughout and paired with a warm and golden Minnesota Kasota stone for the vanity.

The designers also carefully selected elements to enhance comfort, both now and in the future. For softness underfoot, the floor was constructed with additional cushioning between the wood and the concrete subfloor. The shower, outfitted with sleek, custom-made grab bars, can accommodate a wheelchair.

Similarly, the lighting plan was created with aging eyes in mind. "The lighting is designed to be both plentiful and nonglaring," Meyer says. Modern fixtures provide task lighting while closet track lighting is adjustable so it can be moved as needed.

Shelves and rods in the closet are also adjustable, allowing the owners to customize storage. Drawer units, raised off the floor, accommodate shoes underneath.

By combining practical features with sophisticated materials, Meyer and Gillespie designed a bath that is striking and well-suited for everyday living. "We really want the homeowners to feel at home here no matter what their age," Gillespie says. 🆂🆂

IN BEAUTIFUL STYLE

- USE METAL ACCENTS TO GIVE WOOD SURFACES A MODERN EDGE.
- BUILD COMPARTMENTS FOR THE TOILET AND SHOWER TO SIMPLIFY BATHROOM SHARING.
- CELEBRATE DETAILS SUCH AS INTEGRATED TOWEL BARS AND RADIATOR SYSTEMS OVER THE WINDOWS THAT KEEP THE BATHROOM TOASTY.

Tranquil
influence

A minimalist sensibility makes for peaceful harmony and free-flowing comfort in a bath without borders.

Opposite: "I chose these sinks because they were pretty and introduced a feminine element into the neutral space," homeowner Katy Boone says of the above-counter fixtures.
This Photo: A frosted-glass panel rises from a wooden ledge behind the vanity counter. The panel is backlit by windows set high on the wall in the dining room.

This Photo: A spacious shower located on the wall opposite the tub features a teak bench that stands up to the spray.
Opposite: Set in a tiled deck, the tub is meant for soaking away one's cares in steamy waters. In keeping with the owner's less-is-more philosophy, the bath's one window remains undressed.

With no barriers to block views, light, or footsteps, homeowner Katy Boone's master bath lives larger than its dimensions. Varying shades of gray and frosty white evoke a sense of Zen-like tranquillity, while allowing thoroughly modern contours and conveniences in the ample-size room to shine.

"I wanted it to be very neutral and contemporary, and it ended up with an Asian feel," says Katy, also an interior designer. "My father was an architect who once lived in Japan—this bath has the neat, minimal, soothing look of Japanese homes that I saw pictures of when I was a child. It's the subtle variations in the small gray tiles that give the room a sense of serenity and a big look."

The 1-inch tiles cover the walls, soaking tub surround, and vanity, and allow the eye to move freely about the bath's unfettered environs. The room's design and color palette echo those found throughout the two-room, two-story Mount Pleasant, South Carolina, home Katy built three years ago. The master bedroom and bath occupy a loftlike space that is half the size of the floor below.

Sunlight shared with the adjoining bedroom and the rooms below streams unblocked over glass partitions and through windows and wide doorways. Frosted-glass panels enclose the commode while a like-minded glass panel rises behind the vanity to create a partial wall that invites illumination from the windows set high on the first floor's dining room walls that reach to the second story.

In keeping with Katy's preferences for rooms free of doors and walls, the bath's interior seamlessly segues from vanity to soaking tub to open shower.

"When you're in the open shower, there's natural light dancing all around you," says Katy. "It's definitely a space that's soothing in its simplicity."

...tile Allure

*B*athrooms are nothing if not about relaxation. Steam showers and spa-like amenities aside, today's baths are an extension of a home's living spaces. Envision comfy chairs nestled by a fireplace, shelves lined with books, and soft rugs underfoot. Such indulgences maximize the pleasure. So sit back and relax. Your bath welcomes you to linger!

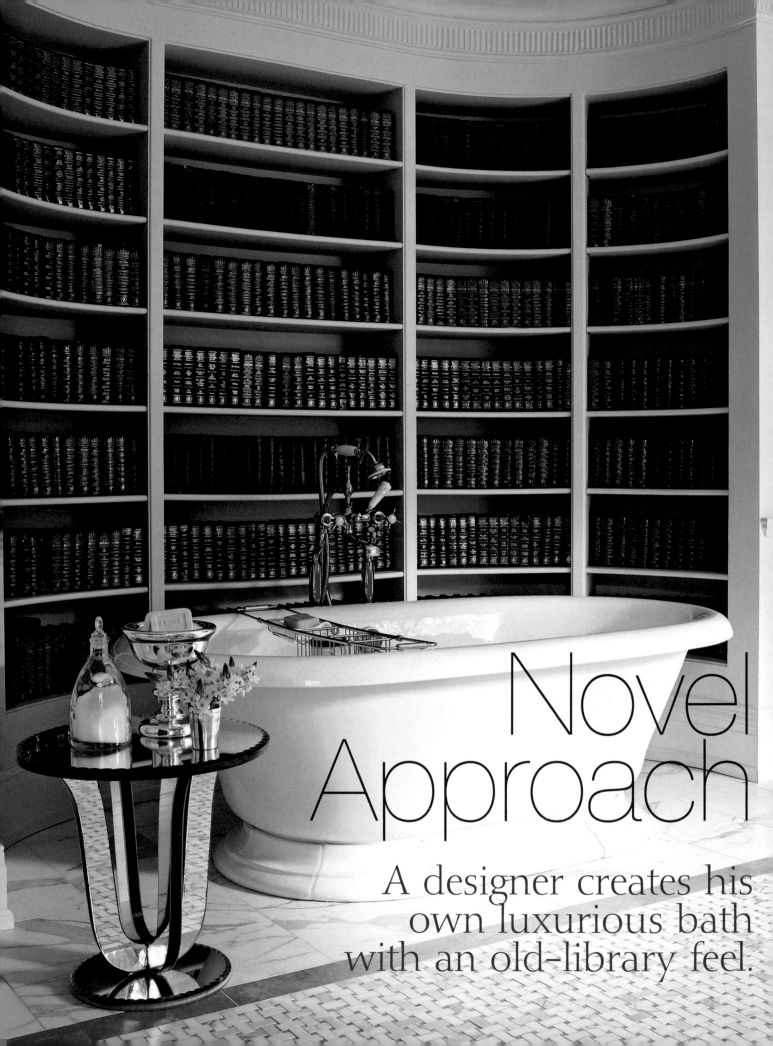

Novel Approach

A designer creates his own luxurious bath with an old-library feel.

*W*With oversize cozy chairs flanking the fireplace and a dramatic niche lined with floor-to-ceiling shelves of leather-bound books, Toronto interior designer Brian Gluckstein's bath looks more like a salon. "I wanted more than a bath," he says of the room he designed for himself and partner Gary Sarantopoulos. "I truly wanted a retreat."

His approach was to borrow elements from the home's more traditional living spaces to achieve comfort and sophistication not usually associated with a bath. The tub's library niche was his first departure from traditional design.

"I have always loved old libraries," Brian says. "I never made the connection between libraries and baths until I saw a bath in a London townhouse with a tiny bookcase in it."

In his own bath, he expanded on this idea and used the bookcase to carve out an intimate bathing area. Featuring a dramatic curve, the built-in bookcase mirrors the form of the tub. "I wanted the tub in a little alcove so it felt cozier," Brian says. The design also affords a practical benefit. "You can read a story while in the tub and then place the book back on the shelf," he says. (His collection is heavy on short story anthologies.)

While the tub functions almost as a piece of sculpture, the rest of the bathroom's utilitarian items are well disguised. A shower room and water closet are tucked behind doors on

Above: Paneled walls, a marble mosaic on the floor, a pair of easy chairs, and a built-in bookcase bring the comforts of a sophisticated living room to Brian Gluckstein's Toronto bath.
Opposite: A built-in bookcase forms a cozy alcove for a classic freestanding tub. "I didn't really want it to feel like a bath," Brian says. "I wanted it to feel like a study."

RUG-PATTERN FLOOR MOSAICS
create a living room feel in the bath, where
textiles are impractical. A dark border best
frames the illusion of layers.

either side of the tub. An unfitted vanity, designed to resemble an English campaign chest, anchors one end of the room with dark mahogany, a Calcutta marble top, and nickel-plated hardware. Brian eschewed traditional sconces in favor of a pair of lamps on the vanity top.

Fireside seating completes the bath's focus on salon comforts. Brian chose a Georgian-inspired fireplace mantel that matches other details in the 1915 house and then added paneling to enhance its architectural stature. On the floor, he used a mix of marble tile to create a faux rug that breaks up the surrounding white surfaces.

Long panels of thick, white terry cloth hang over the room's French doors, adding softness to the room's many hard surfaces and lending privacy when needed. An unexpected choice, the material's texture is at once eye-catching and inviting. "It almost drapes like velvet," Brian says.

Terry cloth gracefully covers the club chairs near the fireplace as well. Sitting in the chairs, one can almost imagine being enveloped in a warm towel after a relaxing bath. "Terry

cloth is so thick and wonderful. People love wrapping themselves in it," Brian says. "I took the idea of the big, fluffy towel one step further."

The material is just one ingredient Brian uses to achieve a relaxed sense of luxury. His formula is simple: Use fine materials and comfortable furniture in an unpretentious way. "While the room (15×18 feet) is larger than most, it feels warm and welcoming," Brian says. "I love a spa-like space, a truly private environment where someone can find a peaceful moment in the midst of a busy life."

Above: Brian modeled the vanity after an English campaign chest, seeking a look that was somewhat masculine and not overly detailed. Dark mahogany provides bold contrast with surrounding planes of white.
Opposite: Georgian-style details on the fireplace mantel are repeated throughout the bath in crown molding. Club chairs add a sense of comfort, enhanced by terry cloth upholstery and gray suede trim.

This Photo: A clean palette combines with classical millwork and European elegance.
Opposite: Louvered doors lead to a relaxing veranda.

Coastal Reflections

A classical bath embraces
the ambience of seaside views.

Left: Graceful curves soften the vanities and backsplash. Reflective crystal pulls, faucets, and Venetian mirrors add formal flair.
Opposite: Comfortable chairs and a softly hued Oriental rug create a well-nested look to complement the furniture-style vanities.

The Jacksonville, Florida, master bath of Terri and Mac McGehee offers a serene view of moss-draped oaks, pines, and magnolias. Ospreys, herons, and ducks dart and glide on St. John's River, and an occasional bald eagle soars. As the weather's mood changes, so do the coastline's hues. "The river is blue in sunlight, light gray during times of bright clouds, and dark gray during storms," Terri says. The couple's bath, featuring the sparkle of a Calcutta marble mosaic floor and ocean-blue walls, responds to broad views of sky and water with classical repose.

"The sandy-hue marble communicates quiet elegance," says the room's architect, David Case. "It gleams, and the light seems to hit it differently every time." The luxurious expanse of marble also reflects the room's poise on the upper level of a traditional, Georgian-style home. Connected to a breezy, fully furnished veranda via plantation-style shuttered doors, the bath's many refinements mingle with the ease of outdoor living.

Casual airs stem from the addition of comfortable armchairs slipcovered in white cotton canvas, as well as the simple design of raised-panel cabinetry. Towels rest on a gilded iron-scrollwork étagère whose form resembles an outdoor plant stand.

Yet elegance prevails due to the room's formal symmetry. The bath's floor plan is organized around the central axis of a pilaster-lined hallway leading to a progression of task niches: a shower opposite a commode room, two dressing areas, and two closets.

Above: The mosaic-tile floor continues into the shower stall.
Opposite: Crystal-beaded light fixtures hang at opposite ends of the mirrored hall connecting distinct task areas.
Right: A nook off the central hall serves as a cozy spot for this neoclassic-style dressing table.

In addition to enhancing the room's flow, the hall establishes a fixed sight line that leads to the freestanding soaking tub, perched prominently under the room's large, central window. A floor-to-ceiling mirror at the hall's opposite end reflects the shapely tub and overhead chandelier for echoes of European-style elegance.

Just as the layout orients bathers to views past the tub, Case and interior designer Terrie Schneider were careful to lend the bath's central windows weight and definition. Case set off each window with simple, clean-lined pilasters painted a crisp white and grouped for rhythm. "They have the same mass and proportion as Palladian windows but without the arch," he says. Elsewhere, Schneider added white shutters for privacy, but above

the tub she opted to leave the panes bare "because that river view is our primary focal point," she says

Venetian mirrors above the twin marble-topped vanities reflect the bath's coastal views as well as a delicate European approach to glamour. Oval sinks, arched backsplashes, and curvy bowfront cabinets are additional custom touches adding soft counterpoint to the room's strong verticals and horizontals.

"This is the room where Mac and I begin and end our day," says Terri. "It's so much more than a utilitarian place to clean up and brush teeth. It's our refuge."

Southern Hospitality

A genteel Low Country bath combines history with modern convenience.

*S*teeping themselves in the graceful architecture and lazy-day charm of Beaufort, South Carolina, Graham and Anne Denton grew rapt in details. Their appreciation focused on the timeworn millwork, wide-plank floors, and softly flickering gas lamps of the city's antebellum mansions—features they borrowed in their nearby Spring Island, South Carolina, master bath. "We were after that Old Southern character—the simplicity, the beauty," Graham says. "Yet we also needed the space to serve our contemporary needs."

Architect Jim Strickland weaved this gracious sense of history into the new bath's design. "The house is a simple Georgian Federal, so it didn't need marble floors and an enormous tub," he says. Instead, he fashioned a modest-size corridor with honest, hand-crafted details. Warmed by salvaged heart-pine flooring, the crisply paneled room has a clean look desirable today, while period fixtures and antique-inspired hardware send it gliding back in time.

Amenities subtly abound, including a morning kitchen. Tucked between the bath and a walk-in closet, it's a place for the Dentons to pick up the day's first splash of coffee. Though clearly a modern luxury, the kitchen radiates nostalgia thanks to the historical styling of its paneling, trim, and a cupboard that conceals appliances.

Strickland and designer Ruth Edwards used this same architectural treatment, which included a combination of vintage moldings and humble materials, throughout the bath, always with an eye toward restraint. "We went very, very simple with the woodwork," Strickland says, for example, eschewing multiple levels of trim. What appears to be expensive molding is instead the mirror reflection of simple pencil molds, a clever sleight of hand he relishes.

Symmetry from dual vanities and a single window, cozied with a bench seat, lends authenticity to the design. "All line up on an axis," Strickland says. "That's so important for a traditional look."

Also vital, he insists, is proper scale. "Old buildings are beautiful when balanced and appropriate," Strickland says. "This space feels old because it's well-fitted, both to the house and to every little detail." 🛁

Above: Antique gas fixtures, converted to electric, add a hint of long-ago gentility.
Left: White tiles and a frameless glass door ensure that the shower doesn't command attention.
Opposite: Slim mirrored cabinets and drawers help the sink look like a piece of built-in furniture.

Best of Both Worlds

Fire and water provide elegant indulgence.

Opposite and Above: For a classic look, this bath takes a back-to-basics approach to materials. Subway tile, white woodwork, and honed marble are timeless elements. A graveled terrace is an adjunct to the bath, a place to relax while the tub fills.

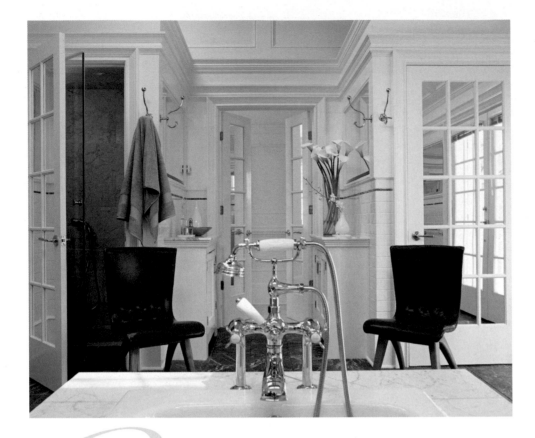

*C*ombining traditional architectural ornament with thoroughly modern notions of comfort and convenience, this Connecticut bath is a sumptuous sanctuary for homeowners Dennis Kyte and Seymour Surnow. "You can spend a good part of a Sunday in there to rejuvenate for the week ahead," Dennis says. "It's almost like having your own spa."

Furniturelike linen cabinets flanking the entry vestibule provide an indication of the kind of opulence that awaits within. The first elements that come into view—an antique wrought-iron French chandelier suspended from a pitched ceiling that soars to 20 feet, a pair of sassy retro red leather chairs, and a jetted tub encased in Italian marble—exude VIP status.

"If there is such a thing, that is a masculine chandelier," says Dennis, a designer and home builder. "Because it's almost monumental and has crystals the size of goose eggs, it gives you a hint of what you're about to experience—pampering and relaxation on a grand scale."

The tub is the center of it all, sited below a two-story bank of divided-light windows and flanked by console sinks with marble countertops. "Having a tub in the middle of a room, rather than in a typical alcove, allows you to relax and enjoy what's around you," Dennis says. "In this case, that's a blazing fireplace to one side and, to the other, French doors that open onto a graveled terrace. Invariably, when we entertain, I find dames in cocktail dresses sitting on the edge of that tub as if it were an outdoor fountain."

Above a wainscoting of pristine subway tiles, panels of beveled mirror encircle the room. "It wasn't an attempt

Pages 160–161 and Opposite: Sunk into a marble-paneled surround and drenched with daylight, a whirlpool tub is clearly the star. Flames in a gas fireplace flicker through a pyramid of stone balls. Highly collectible chairs from the '50s and a coffee table from the '60s reflect a preference for retro furnishings.
Above: In the bathroom's entry vestibule, built-in linen cabinets look like pieces of finely crafted furniture. On either side, behind mirrored French doors, are separate compartments for a marble-lined steam shower and a toilet.

Above: In a context of classic architecture, humble antique barn beams and a haughty French chandelier are eccentric accents that provide one-of-kind appeal.
Opposite: Against a subway-tiled wainscoting, marble-topped console sinks stand elegantly on crystal legs.

to make the space seem larger, rather to make it almost transparent," Dennis says. "It's as if you're looking through the walls because what you see is a reflection of the fire in the fireplace or the greenery outside. And, because the daylight is constantly changing, the views change constantly, too."

Interior and exterior vistas are also reflected in the mirrored French doors of the room's twin "pavilions," one of which is a toilet compartment and the other a cleverly concealed steam shower. Both are lavishly layered with millwork. "I wanted the shower and the loo to be less than obvious to someone enjoying a nice, long soak in the tub, so I built little boxes for each of them," Dennis says. "With the doors closed, they are beautiful pieces of classic architecture, yet every bit as utilitarian as if the fixtures were exposed."

Above it all, massive antique chestnut barn beams temper the bath's architectural refinement with a note of rusticity. The beams and the honed-marble tiles imply longevity.

"The marble gives the floor a well-worn look," Dennis says. "Along with all the traditional woodwork and the French doors, it conveys the impression that the room has a long history of pampering people and continues to do that exceedingly well." ◼

IN BEAUTIFUL STYLE

- GIVE CUSTOM CABINETRY THE LOOK OF FINE FURNITURE WITH MOLDINGS AND SPECIAL FINISHES.
- TRANSFORM A BATHROOM INTO A SPA BY PAIRING THE TUB WITH A FIREPLACE.
- ADD A PERSONAL NOTE BY COMBINING FAVORITES — ELEGANT MARBLE WITH '50S LEATHER CHAIRS — IN ONE SPACE.

Suite Sophisticate

Lavish amenities and dapper details bring a newly built bath vintage glamour.

Opposite: A glass wall behind the soaking tub exposes the travertine-tiled shower, adding midtone hues to the bath's high-contrast palette of dark woods against white marble. **This Photo:** The bath's layout leaves one paneled wall free to accommodate artwork and a freestanding dressing table.

In dreaming up ways to capture the allure of Old Hollywood for one of her projects—a master bath in a stately Houston home—designer Kelly Welsh couldn't shake the image of Cary Grant. The actor's dapper style and smooth-as-silk demeanor exemplified the romance of decades past, when white-gloved ladies sipped champagne and elegance was de rigueur.

"The look is classic 1940s and a bit nostalgic, but with modern details," says Welsh, a principal designer with Bellacasa Design Associates. "We envisioned the bath melding traditional and contemporary styles, with subtle vintage touches and a soothing atmosphere." They also sought to raise architectural interest in the space while softening the effects of its grand scale. One solution: rich walnut-stained paneling reminiscent of a gentleman's den.

Finely tailored panels soar beneath the room's 17-foot ceilings, creating warmth, character, and a mainstay for the decor. "That was our starting point," Welsh says. "Once the paneling was in place, it was a matter of building contrast and texture."

The designers countered the walnut's richness with pale travertine stone and shiny white carrara marble. Washes of aqua paint cover wall space above the panels with barely a hint of color. "The interplay of light and dark adds a sense of drama, and it keeps the room from feeling too heavy," Welsh explains.

Residential designer Robert Dame fashioned the basic layout with a priority on balance. In positioning identical vanities on either side of a window, he lent order and structure to the space. Not all is traditional, however. In lieu of a mirrored back to the soaking tub niche, he opted for a sheet of glass that looks through to the floor-to-ceiling travertine shower. "Placing the tub in front of the glass shower and away from the window, where it's expected, enhances the perceived depth of the room," Dame says. "Plus, it allowed us to make a television viewable from the shower."

Right: Pale-hue and floral-pattern fabrics adorning the window seat offset the bath's hard surfaces, infusing the space with a wisp of softness.

Such amenities encourage lingering. Below the garden-facing window, Dame designed a bench seat, cozy for reading, while across the room he reserved space for Welsh to place a dressing table. "Real furniture gives personality to a bath," Welsh says.

The key to integrating furnishings with the room's architectural design is simplicity. The crisp, clean lines of millwork allowed Welsh's team to explore more sinuous shapes in freestanding furnishings. Likewise for the lighting and fixtures: While two beaded chandeliers add a touch of glitz, simple sconces and cross-handle knobs on the plumbing fixtures show modesty. "That's how we grounded the space," Welsh says. "The bath has a wonderful, opulent, luxury-hotel look, but it also feels comfortable."

This Photo: Classical symmetry
defines the dual vanities,
connected by a cozy window seat.

This Photo: The dressing area doubles as a lounge. A bureau-styled built-in sits between mirrored closet doors.
Opposite: French doors echo the styling of the dressing area's closet doors.

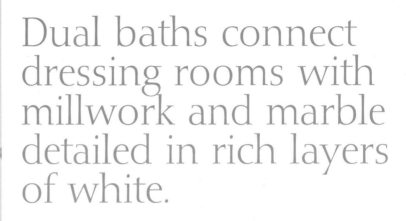

Dual baths connect
dressing rooms with
millwork and marble
detailed in rich layers
of white.

Masterful Union

FRENCH DOORS used in lieu of windows
open an upper-level bath to
the clouds. A thick ledge and a decorative
balconette—à la vintage European hotels—
completes the design.

Right: The pale gray marble of a vanity counter continues into a low backsplash.
Below: Mirrors are sited to bounce light and reflections over the tub and its cloudlike scheme of whites with gray marble decking.
Opposite: One bath features a luxurious tub. Paneled doors separate the room from other spaces and French doors open the room to breezes.

Small spaces just feel cozier than one large one. It's a conviction shared by the homeowners of this bath who chose to divvy an extensive bath suite into intimate rooms. The plan sites a couple's small baths, one for each, between designated dressing rooms. Exquisitely detailed millwork and expanses of white and pale gray marble flow from room to room, unifying the suite in a somewhat classic, almost minimal esthetic.

"The design has a continuous theme and variations, much like music," says project supervisor Rob Philabaum of G.M. Hunt, Inc., builders in Scottsdale, Arizona, who helped the homeowner execute her vision. Moldings, for instance, change from baroque to minimal profiles while keeping to a consistent aesthetic. "The homeowner is a master at this,"

Philabaum says. "I've never seen anyone with a more incredible eye for detail. She can visualize very slight changes in depth, width, spacing."

Inspiration for the suite's design ranged from the unique character of collected antiques to photos gathered by the homeowners during visits to Italy and France over a 10-year period. White links these disparate influences, and, like the geometric inlay on Greek marble floors, is key to evoking classic architecture. The color brings crisp definition to details so carefully wrought.

Equal attention was paid to beauty and everyday function—a chair to hold towels, a sink console wide enough for a cup of coffee. Whether discussing ceiling heights, molding profiles, or muntin widths, Philabaum remained open to the

homeowner's keen eye to determine the best proportions. When existing pieces proved too thick or too slight, they had nickel-plated legs for the wall-mount vanity custom-made.

Cabinetry also received great attention. The dual baths are entered via dressing areas that serve to establish the style of millwork throughout the suite. A built-in in the husband's bath masquerades as a bureau, while a wall of recessed paneled doors enclose storage akin to bedroom closets. All are finished with carefully researched reproduction escutcheons and knobs that hearken back to the 1930s, a period the homeowner enjoys for its simply stated elegance.

Storage is nearly always enclosed for a clutter-free look. The result is dressing areas so serene, the homeowner decided hers should also serve for lounging. She added a vintage French recamier in the center of the room, where she can put her feet up, maybe read a book. Also at her request, the suite's marble floors stop at her dressing room's door, ceding to the plush comfort of dove-gray carpet.

Such relaxing airs are accentuated by a host of windows and French doors, each exquisitely crafted by a local woodworker. All open out in vintage European style, yet are cleverly fitted with shutters that tuck neatly away into walls on recessed sliding tracks.

There's a romance to it all, especially when breezes flow through French doors opened at the foot of the tub. Every detail adds purpose, not to mention layers of character. 🏠

Refined for Relaxing

A couple-friendly floor plan
includes spalike comforts
and a classical countenance.

Opposite: The faucets and light fixtures bear an oil-rubbed bronze finish, linking them to the bronze inset tiles on the floor and shower walls.
This Photo: At the island, countertops on both sides of the center mirrors provide space for toiletries.

" I wanted to create a European-style bath that was serene and peaceful."

DESIGNER TINA BARCLAY

Form and function were always at the top of interior designer Tina Barclay's mind, as she stretched a 15×16-foot space in a Portland, Oregon, showhouse to its very limits. With a central island created by back-to-back vanities, the master bathroom holds a surprising wealth of stay-awhile amenities, ranging from an in-bath coffee bar to a freestanding soaking tub with remote-controlled whirlpool jets to a spacious shower that lies within reach of a towel-warming drawer.

"By placing the island in the center, it allowed me to tuck more things into the space," Barclay notes. "Instead of walking across miles of empty floor in a large bath, why not use the center for an island? That way you don't have to line up everything along the perimeter. Like in a kitchen, an island breaks up the space and makes it more interesting."

Barclay's design mission was twofold: to create a self-contained retreat that accommodated a couple's grooming, bathing, and relaxation needs, and to fill it to the brim with sophisticated European character.

Barclay says she wanted to create a space that would be a luxurious suite in itself—with all the amenities of a hotel. "It's very ethereal, with honed limestone, bronze tiles, and very serene and cool with sage-green walls that are a watery color like that of an old Coke bottle," she says.

Almost monochromatic in scheme, the master bath relies on subtle shifts in natural hues, earthen textures, and painted finishes for its appreciable appeal. Cabinets glazed to look antique lend a

Opposite: Throughout the bath, polished granite countertops turn up the shimmer quotient and mirror the colors ingrained in the honed limestone flooring.
Above: A towel-warming drawer, operating much like a warming drawer found in a kitchen, heats up the spa-like spirit of this considerably indulgent space. Just steps from the limestone-tiled shower and the central vanity island, the drawer supplies toasty after-shower and post-shaving wraps.

Left: Reclining in the freestanding tub, homeowners take in verdant views of vineyards, pastures, and hillsides through a wall of windows. A row of transom windows above invites even more sunlight. Lotus-pattern, solid-bronze tiles give the checkerboard floor a visual lift.
Below: Placed at the intersections of larger tiles, bronze accents brighten the limestone.

timeless European air while supplying a soft-edged counterpoint to the lustrous density of the granite countertops. Glass doors on the cabinets promote a light and airy openness while showcasing colorful accessories, ranging from candles and bath salts to coffee cups and bath towels.

Three-inch-square solid-bronze tiles inset in the checkerboard floor and shower walls add a powerful punch to the stone-on-stone design. "The bronze tiles are artful and interesting, and cause you to stop and notice different elements in the room," the designer says.

The bath's focal point, the built-for-two island, is defined by an overmantel composed of architecturally detailed columns. The columns hold a pair of mirrors and hide electrical wires that power the vanity lights. By moving the sinks to the center of the room, Barclay was able to include a multidrawer dressing table.

"It really is an optimal master bathroom design," Barclay says. "It's not only beautiful in form but highly functional. It illustrates that you can have all the amenities you want right in your bathroom."

This Photo: A coffee bar on a wall near the entry to the bedroom completes the self-sufficient suite. Whether they want a cup of coffee or a bedtime snack, the homeowners have the conveniences at hand.

This Photo: This wall-less bath is a comfortably furnished extension of the master bedroom suite.
Opposite: Ebonized wood adds sharp contrast to the vanity, whose geometry and clean, contemporary lines update the farm-style sink.

From Bed

to Bath Wide-open spaces bring modern versatility to a farmhouse bath.

Stacey and David Schieffelin's master bathroom reveals a host of distinguishing features, including custom tilework; wooden beams original to the couple's Woodbury, Connecticut, farmhouse; and an overhead shower fixture that simulates tropical rain. But the bath's most unique element is what's not there: a wall dividing it from the master bedroom. Instead, the bath is an integral part of a multipurpose retreat.

"It's our home spa, reading area, and a light-filled conversation area," Stacey says. "In this antique home, there are plenty of small, private spaces. Here we preferred an open bath-bedroom feeling."

Stacey and David moved from the bustle of Manhattan to the quiet of this historic home, which was built before 1720 on land deeded in 1677. They created the bedroom-bath suite during a whole-house remodeling by removing a wall between two former bedrooms. As contractors tore down paneling, they discovered large antique support beams, which the Schieffelins used to determine an 8×14-foot area for the bath.

Because the open plan is typical of a more contemporary lifestyle than the home's historical architecture suggests, bathroom designer Jennifer Black opted for a design that juxtaposes old and new. She decided on modern-style bath fixtures whose clean lines and sharp geometry add counterpoint.

Working without walls, Black delineated the bath's floor space with tile. Dime-size tiles run like a river between the two vanities, abruptly abutting the room's stained plank floor. Color also plays

Left: Antique chairs upholstered in linen with box-pleated skirts offer places to relax. Symmetry and soft colors give the open bath a feeling of harmony. Original beams were left exposed for extra character.

This Photo: A mosaic-tile border in a subtle, running bond pattern draws the eye from the open bath to the adjoining shower room. An interior glass-block window illuminates both spaces with shared light.

Above: To create the feeling of an open-air shower in a confined space, the owners chose frameless glass doors, a glass-block window for light and privacy, and white tiles with a high glaze to reflect light.

Above: Open shelving and a window seat anchor the bath's seating area while juxtaposing crisp geometry against classic features such as a half demilune window and skirted upholstery on a wing chair.

a defining role. Watery blues and greens paired with bright white create a scheme that contrasts with the warm wood hues of the sleeping area. The separate shower room is all white with soft blue-gray accents and glass-block windows that let in additional light.

The bath's use of white "makes the space seem larger and more open," Stacey says, "while highlighting the architectural styling of the windows, bookcases, marble floors, and porcelain bath fixtures." The designer's addition of black accents against the light backdrop injects contemporary punch. Both vanity bases feature an ebonized finish to match dark wood frames on mirrors as well as the support for a freestanding tub.

The focal point tub anchors the bath's symmetrical design and sets a mood of relaxed comfort. An updated version of familiar claw-foot models, its style makes a contemporary nod to the room's farmhouse beginnings. The fixture's low, spacious

proportions were customized for the space; originally on high pedestals, the tub was cut down to sit beneath the sill of an oversize multipane window, a perfect spot for enjoying a relaxing soak or for the couple to watch their two young daughters make a game of bath time in the morning light.

For a greater sense of retreat, the bath includes two comfortable wing chairs and a small side table, creating an intimate area for reading or conversation. Here Stacey can sit and talk to the girls during bath time, reviewing the day and helping turn the space into "the most-used area in the house," she says.

The clean, comfortable haven proves that even a historical master bath can be redefined for modern, multitasking days. "We have a very busy home," Stacey says. "The bath area should be a place of peace and privacy to indulge in a candlelit soak while being free to dream." ❧

Resources

Every beautiful bath starts with planning and vision. The design professionals listed here are largely responsible for the elegant and efficient spaces featured in this book. If none are in your area, check phone listings for local design firms. Stores that sell bath fixtures may also offer design services.

CLASSIC ELEGANCE

NECESSARY INDULGENCE
Pages: 8–13
Architect: Stephen Fuller, 4179 Pleasant Hill Rd., Duluth, GA 30096; 800/274-2444; *stephenfuller.com.*
Interior designer: Brian Gluckstein, ARIDO, ASID, IDC, Gluckstein Design Planning, 234 Davenport Rd., Toronto, ON M5R 1J6 Canada; 416/928-2067; *glucksteindesign.com.*

CLEARLY STATED GRACE
Pages: 14–17
Architects: Robert McAlpine, principal, and Scott Torode, project architect, McAlpine Tankersley Architecture, 1 Dexter Ave., Montgomery, AL 36104; 334/262-8315; *mcalpinetankersley.com.*
Interior designer: Jane Schwab, Circa Interiors &

Antiques, 2321 Crescent Ave., Charlotte, NC 28207; 704/332-6369; e-mail: circainteriors@aol.com.

NEW-WORLD POLISH
Pages: 18–21
Architect: Doug Walter, AIA, Doug Walter Architects, 280 Columbine St., Suite 205, Denver, CO 80206; 303/320-6916.
Project manager: Hamid Khellaf, Doug Walter Architects, 280 Columbine St., Suite 205, Denver, CO 80206; 303/320-6916.
Interior designers: Judy Gubner, ASID, and Colleen Johnson, ASID, In-Site Design Group, Inc., 1280 S. Clayton St., Denver, CO 80210; 303/691-9000.

EASY MEETS ELEGANT
Pages: 22-27
Architect: Hanna Gabriel Wells, 4993 Niagara Ave.,

GRAND STATEMENTS

BOLD AND BEAUTIFUL
Pages: 80-85
Architects: Bill Harrison, AIA, and Dawn Bennett, AIA, Harrison Design Associates, 3198 Cains Hill Place NW, Suite 200, Atlanta, GA 30305; 404/365-7760; harrisondesignassociates.com.
Interior designer: Shon Parker, Shon Parker Design, Atlanta; 404/784-7463; shonparkerdesign.com.

EVERYDAY EDEN
Pages: 86-91
Architect: John Krasnodebski, Lake Forest Landmark Development Co., Lake Forest, Illinois; 847/615-0637.
Residential designer: Kris Boyaris, Lake Forest Landmark Development Co., Lake Forest, Illinois; 847/615-0637.

VINTAGE DECEPTION
Pages: 92-97
Bath designer: Lois Kennedy, CKD, Portfolio Kitchens, Vienna, Virginia; 703/242-0330; portfoliokitchens.com.
Interior designer: Barry Darr Dixon, Barry Dixon, Inc., 8394 Elway Lane, Warrenton, VA 20186; 540/341-8501; barrydixon.com.

AIR OF ANTIQUITY
Pages: 98-103
Interior designer: Marjorie Carter, ASID, Blueberry Hill, Dublin, New Hampshire.

GETTING INTO CHARACTER
Pages: 104-107
Designers: Martha Angus and Susan Wicks, Martha Angus, LLC, 1017 Bush St., San Francisco, CA 94109; 415/931-8060; marthaangus.com.

SLEEK SOPHISTICATION

PACIFIC CALM
Pages: 110-113
Interior designers: David Rivera, ASID, CID, and Eugene Nahemow, CID, Nahemow Rivera Group, LLC, 486 Eighth St., San Francisco, CA 94103; 415/621-7236; nahemowriveragroup.com.

DRAMATICALLY INCLINED
Pages: 114-121
Architect: Steve Rankin, Steve Rankin Architecture, 470 49th St., Oakland, CA 94609; 510/653-2534.

TURNING EAST
Pages: 122-127
Residential designer: Ralph Hoffman, MAP Lab, Inc., 1837 W. Fulton St., Chicago, IL 60612; 312/432-0870; maplab.com.
Interior designer: Chris Garrett, Garrett Paschen, Ltd., 409 Greenwood St., Evanston, IL 60201; 847/866-6999; garrettpaschen.com.

SPARE ESSENTIALS
Pages: 128-131
Architect: Margaret McCurry, FAIA, Tigerman & McCurry Architects, 444 N. Wells St., Suite 206, Chicago, IL 60610; 312/644-5880; tigerman-mccurry.com.

SHEER STRENGTH
Pages: 132-137
Architect: Thomas Meyer, FAIA, MS+R Architects, Ltd., 710 S. Second St., Minneapolis, MN 55401; 612/375-0336; msrltd.com.
Interior designer: Jodi Gillespie, ASID, MS+R Architects, Ltd., 710 S. Second St., Minneapolis, MN 55401; 612/375-0336; msrltd.com.

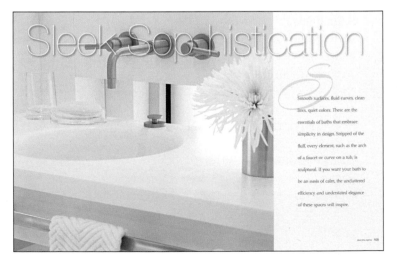

STAY-AWHILE ALLURE

NOVEL APPROACH
Pages: 144–147
Interior designer: Brian Gluckstein, ARIDO, ASID, IDC, Gluckstein Design Planning, 234 Davenport Rd., Toronto, ON M5R 1J6 Canada; 416/928-2067; *gluckstindesign.com.*

COASTAL REFLECTIONS
Pages: 148–153
Architect: David Case, Richard Skinner & Associates, Architects, 2245 St. Johns Ave., Jacksonville, FL 32205; 904/387-6710; *rs-architects.com.*
Interior designer: Terry Schneider, T. Schneider Interior Design, Jacksonville, Florida.

SOUTHERN HOSPITALITY
Pages: 154–157
Architect: Jim Strickland, Historical Concepts, Peachtree City, Georgia; 770/487-6737; *historicalconcepts.com.*
Interior designer: Ruth Edwards, Ruth Edwards Antiques and Interiors, Hilton Head Island, South Carolina; 843/671-2223.

BEST OF BOTH WORLDS
Pages: 158–165
Residential designer: Dennis Kyte, Dennis Kyte, Inc., Washington Depot, Connecticut; e-mail: dkyte@snet.net.

SUITE SOPHISTICATE
Pages: 166–169
Interior designer: Kelly Welsh, Bellacasa Design Associates, Inc., 4200 Research Forest, Suite 350; The Woodlands, TX 77381; 281/419-5550; *bellacasadesign. com.*

MASTERFUL UNION
Pages: 170–175
Architects: Mark Candelaria, Candelaria Design Associates, LLC, 4450 N. 12th St., Suite 278, Phoenix, AZ 85014; 877/923-4232; *candelariadesign.com;* and Oz Group, 6615 N. Scottsdale Rd., Suite 200; Scottsdale, AZ 85250; 480/443-4904; *ozarchitects.com.*

REFINED FOR RELAXING
Pages: 176–181
Interior designers: Eric Schnell, Alan Mascord Design Associates, Inc., 1305 NW. 18th Ave., Portland, OR 97209; 800/411-0231; *mascord.com;* and Tina Barclay, Allied Member ASID, Barclay Interior Design Group, 3 Monroe Pkwy., Suite P-253; Lake Oswego, OR 97035; 503/635-1278; *barclayinteriors.com.*

find
your
style

Decorative
paint
Techniques & Ideas

BATH
Design Guide

NEW **COLOR SCHEMES MADE EASY**

POPULAR PALETTES FOR EVERY ROOM

The **elements** of **your style** can be found in great
decorating books from **Better Homes and Gardens**®

ADT1043_0908